A New Heaven, A New Earth

CATHOLICITY IN AN EVOLVING UNIVERSE

A New Heaven, A New Earth

The Bible and Catholicity

DIANNE BERGANT

ORBIS BOOKS

Maryknoll, New York 10545

ORBIS BOOKS
Maryknoll, New York 10545

Fathers and Brothers
MARYKNOLL™

Founded in 1970, Orbis Books endeavors to publish works that enlighten the mind, nourish the spirit, and challenge the conscience. The publishing arm of the Maryknoll Fathers and Brothers, Orbis seeks to explore the global dimensions of the Christian faith and mission, to invite dialogue with diverse cultures and religious traditions, and to serve the cause of reconciliation and peace. The books published reflect the views of their authors and do not represent the official position of the Maryknoll Society. To learn more about Maryknoll and Orbis Books, please visit our website at www.maryknollsociety.org.

Copyright © 2016 by Dianne Bergant.

Published by Orbis Books, Maryknoll, New York 10545–0302.

Manufactured in the United States of America.

Manuscript editing and typesetting by Joan Weber Laflamme.

Library of Congress Cataloging-in-Publication Data

Bergant, Dianne.
    A new heaven, a new earth : the Bible and catholicity /by Dianne Bergant.
        pages cm. — (Catholicity in an evolving universe series)
        Includes index.
    ISBN 978-1-62698-180-5 (pbk.)
    1. Biblical cosmology. I. Title.
BS651.B347 2016
220.6—dc23

2015028058

Contents

"God so loved the world"

—John 3:16

Introduction

Women and men have always been fascinated by the universe.[1] Poets, dreamers, and mystics of every kind have looked to the heavens in wonder and awe and for inspiration. The magnificence and scope of the universe have transported them to realms of fantasy and ecstasy alike. This universe has both thrilled them and frightened them. They have traced the positions of the stars and uncovered Orion the Hunter; they have recognized the sparks from Thor's hammer in the lightning that streaks through the sky; they have been startled by the voice of YHWH[2] in the thunder that rolls across the heavens; they have experienced the monthly phases of the moon in the life cycle of women. Just as elements of the heavens were ascribed with human characteristics, so people's understanding of the origin, structure, makeup, and working of the universe has influenced how they perceive human nature, its place and role within that universe, and divinity and its power and control over that universe.

---

[1] The passage from the Gospel according to John that serves as the epigraph for this introduction usually is limited in focus to humankind. However, the Greek word translated as "world" is *kósmos—cosmos* or *universe,* in English—which is not so narrowly understood.

[2] YHWH is the particular name of the God of Israel. The ancient Israelites believed that an aspect of an individual's identity is contained in that person's name. Therefore, after the Babylonian exile (ca. 586 BCE), as a sign of respect for God, the divine name was not pronounced and only the consonants of the name were written.

Turning to the Bible we discover that many of the stories that the ancient Israelites told about themselves reveal traces of their understanding of their own origin and their place in the universe. For example, in the first creation story we read that God created a dome to separate the waters (Gen 1:6–8). From passages such as these we see that they believed that Earth[3] was originally covered by chaotic waters. These waters were then separated. The waters above Earth were held in place by a dome. The other waters were gathered under Earth itself. This cosmological perception grew out of the people's experience of the sky, which seemed to form a clear dome from horizon to horizon. The waters above this dome fell down as rain, while those below surged up from sources underground. The people also thought that they lived on Earth with all other creatures, while God ruled from the heavens. Passages found in various psalms provide insight into this cosmological understanding (Pss 2:4; 47:10; 113:5; 123:1).

Throughout the history of human enlightenment, significant revolutionary scientific discoveries have forced new cosmological renderings, and theological revisions have followed this reshaping. Pythagoras's insistence that Earth is a sphere and not flat challenged literal belief that God is enthroned in the heavens above us. Copernicus's heliocentric model of the universe further threatened well-established concepts of divinely determined human dominance in the universe. Darwin's insight into evolutionary processes disputes the notion of the direct creation of humankind. Astounding scientific facts have continued to be uncovered, and corresponding theological reinterpretations have been repeatedly required.

We face such a revolutionary situation today. Cosmologists speak about multiverses containing billions of galaxies, some of which, no doubt, contain planets that are able to support life. How are we to understand the claims of Christology and soteriology in the face of such discoveries? More to the point of this book—how are we to reconcile the findings of contemporary

---

[3] Many ecologists today think of Earth (with a capital "E") as a subject with rights and privileges rather than as an object totally dependent on human beings.

science that is cosmocentric with the religious message of the Bible, when so much of the latter is anthropocentric and appears to be based on a mythological understanding of the universe?

The prevailing worldview today is definitely anthropocentric. According to this perspective the human person is regarded as the focal point of everything and the measure according to which all else is evaluated. An exaggerated form of this point of view maintains that humankind is both the culmination of creation and its ultimate goal. Accordingly, the rest of natural creation is deemed valuable only to the extent that it is useful in furthering human desires, plans, and accomplishments. A great deal of modern progress owes its existence and development to this perspective.

We cannot deny the extraordinary range or the awesome quality of the achievements of human ingenuity. Astounding feats of science and breathtaking works of art have all been realized through creative employment of components of the natural world. However, these amazing accomplishments have often resulted in humans failing to remember that, as remarkable as they themselves are and as marvelous as their undertakings might be, they are first and foremost members of the community of Earth, dependent upon other members of that community for their very survival.

Many people argue that anthropocentric bias is reinforced by the biblical tradition, specifically the Genesis 1 creation narrative, wherein the first man and woman are given the commission to subdue the earth and have dominion over the rest of creation. However, is it possible that this anthropocentric point of view has been imposed by the biblical reader rather than implied by the biblical author? Might biblical traditions in reality incorporate what today we have named the ecojustice aspects of interconnectedness and interdependence, principles overlooked by many contemporary readers who themselves are steeped in an anthropocentric outlook? Retrieving selected passages from the Bible and training the lens of "community of Earth" on them will show that ancient people never doubted their connection with, even total dependence upon, elements of the natural world. In other words, our biblical tradition presumes a community of Earth.

Catholicity

The overarching and interconnecting theme of the series to which this book belongs is *catholicity*, a word that means "universal in extent" or "encompassing all." In the realms of theology and religious identity, *catholic* usually has come to signify what is identifiably separate—as in Catholic Church or Catholic teaching—in contrast to what is Protestant, Jewish, or Islamic. This is almost the reverse of its foremost meaning. In order to counteract this reversal in meaning, we are challenged today to set aside what is sectarian, factional, tribal, or exclusive and embrace a dynamic movement toward universality and wholeness.

As important as this movement is generally, there is a dimension of created reality in which the dynamic does not really move forward toward the fashioning of forms of catholicity. Instead, it is a retrieval of the realization that a form of wholeness is already present, though often overlooked or forgotten. This form of wholeness is the most fundamental dimension of our reality. It is what is referred to here as the community of Earth, a community that comprises everything within our universe. Contemporary science has brought us to realize that everything of Earth has been made of the same stuff as the stars and has been brought forth through the same process of evolution. Humankind's participation within and oneness with all other members of this community is the ultimate experience of catholicity, a catholicity that is universal in extent and encompassing all.

Despite this fundamental catholicity, the nature and grandeur of human accomplishments have led many of us to see humankind as separate from rather than part of the rest of the natural world. A sense of human superiority over the rest of creation has been reinforced by a literal reading of various passages of scripture. The best-known examples of this include:

Subdue . . . and have dominion. (Gen 1:28)

You have made them a little lower than God. (Ps 8:5)

Such thinking has often led us to ascribe no more than instrumental value to other components of Earth, attaching importance to them only when they seem to serve human goals, thus closing our eyes to their inherent intrinsic value. Still, our blindness in this matter has in no way interrupted the ongoing dynamic of interconnectedness operative within all the forces of Earth. This is now painfully evident in situations such as climate change, the consequences of which we are all experiencing; and the pollution of air and water, which has resulted in the extinction of many species and the occurrence of various forms of cancer in human beings. It behooves us to correct our myopic perspective and focus anew on the oneness we share with the rest of Earth creatures, a oneness that already exists.

As this Orbis series seeks to examine the challenges and possibilities of a new understanding of catholicity, it is only right that a critical eye be trained on the Bible, which, according to the Second Vatican Council, is the "primary and perpetual foundation" of all theology (*Dei Verbum*, no. 24). In doing so, we must remember that this revelatory tradition comes to us clothed in human words, images, and symbols that are steeped in the patent anthropocentrism, religio-ethnic partiality, and gender bias of particular cultures and historical periods. It is these very biases that have turned many people away from the biblical teachings, maintaining that such biases limit or prevent the full flourishing of humankind and the community of Earth of which it is a member. At issue is the question of whether or not the biblical writings can be read in a way that their ecosensitive possibilities might once again be realized. Or must the honest searcher set them aside as artifacts of history?

In order to read biblical passages with an appreciation of the community of Earth, two methodological principles come into play: the hermeneutic of suspicion and the hermeneutic of retrieval.[4] Suspicion is necessary lest one uncritically accept the message of the passage without questioning whether the customs,

---

[4] Norman Habel inserts a step between suspicion and retrieval called empathy or identification. He suggests that the reader identify with some aspect of Earth and then read the text from that point of view. However, if one is able to recognize and explicitly acknowledge the intimate connectedness of all members of the community of Earth, such a step might appear artificial and unnecessary. See Norman C. Habel, "Introducing Ecological Hermeneutics," in *Exploring Ecological Hermeneutics*, 1–8 (Atlanta: Society of Biblical Literature, 2008).

behaviors, and values portrayed therein value or devalue Earth. If they value Earth, the message can be retrieved and retained or developed further. If they devalue Earth, the message will be deemed lacking in revelatory significance and set aside, or it might be retrieved and its objectionable meaning be somehow subverted so that the message can still act in a revelatory fashion. The goal here is to develop an Earth consciousness in reading the Bible, an advocacy stand in support of the community of Earth.

Method

The character of the insights gained from reading is dependent upon the methodological approach employed. Today biblical scholars speak of three fundamental approaches, each attentive to a particular aspect of discourse itself. One approach examines what is referred to as the world within the text, that is, the world created by the author. This approach focuses on literary characteristics including form or genre; subgenres such as simile, metaphor, allegory, and so on. Another approach is concerned with the world behind the text, that is, the world of the author. Here the primary focus of examination moves away from the text itself and attempts to recapture aspects of the political, social, religious, or other cultural profile of the time of origin. This approach seeks to uncover the original meaning intended by the author. Finally, in a third approach, the world in front of the text, the world of the reader is the principal concern. In this approach the text is read through a lens determined by the reader. Examples of such a lens include liberation, postcolonialism, feminism, integrity of creation, and so forth. While all reading seeks to uncover the meaning of the text, a text can yield myriad meanings depending upon which approach is chosen. Is the meaning found in the literary creativity of the text itself? Is it the meaning originally intended by the author? Or does it flow from the particular interest of the reader?

This book is meant to be an experiment in hermeneutics. It offers an ecosensitive way of reading the Bible in order to discover what new insights this approach might yield. The approach employed begins with a careful reading of selected passages from the Bible, calling on aspects of literary criticism to discover the basic meaning of the passage (world within the text). Salient political, social, and religious details drawn from the historical world of the author are brought to these literary findings in order to throw more light on the meaning of the passage (world behind the text). However, the principal interest here is the religious relevance of the uncovered meaning of the passage for the contemporary reader (world in front of the text). To this end, the lens through which passages are viewed is meant to uncover facets of the integrity of creation. This lens is fashioned from the ecojustice principles articulated by the Australian ecotheologian Norman Habel and several of his associates:

1. The principle of intrinsic worth which honors the value of Earth and all of its components in themselves and not in their usefulness to human beings.
2. The principle of interconnectedness which recognizes the interdependence of members of the community of Earth.
3. The principle of voice which appreciates the unique way each member of the community of Earth expresses itself.
4. The principle of purpose which claims that all members of the community of Earth have a part in the dynamic cosmic design.
5. The principle of mutual custodianship which acknowledges the role played by each member of the community of Earth in sustaining Earth's delicate balance.
6. The principle of resistance which maintains that Earth itself struggles against its manipulation and exploitation.[5]

Supporting principles such as these not only yield new insights into the biblical narratives, but they also challenge longstanding anthropological and theological presuppositions. Displacing human beings from their assumed place of privilege as pinnacle of creation and situating them firmly within the multifaceted community of Earth reestablishes them as sisters and brothers

---

[5] Norman C. Habel, ed., *The Earth Bible*, vol. 1, *Readings from the Perspective of Earth* (Sheffield, UK: Sheffield Academic Press, 2000), 24.

of other Earth creatures rather than self-interested sovereigns or ruthless profiteers. Genuine respect for the integrity of other creatures and a willingness to live in harmony with them and not simply over them certainly alters our understanding of what it means to be human. The ethical implications of this might change our manner of living on and with Earth as well.

This new anthropological perspective leads us to new ways of understanding and talking about God. It calls us to choose images of a generous and provident creator whose beauty and imagination are manifest in creation rather than a callous retaliator whose honor has been offended by human transgressions and who wields the forces of nature as a punishing club. These new images can evoke sentiments of wonder and praise and gratitude rather than fear and trembling. Espousing the view of the community of Earth is no mean venture.

Community of Earth

These ecojustice principles have contributed to the emergence of the community of Earth concept, which highlights the interdependence among all natural creation. This concept is not new. In *A Sand County Almanac*, published in 1949, the great ecologist Aldo Leopold speaks about the interconnectedness of all elements within an ecosystem: "The land ethic simply enlarges the boundaries of the community to include soils, waters, plants, and animals, or collectively: the land."[6] Leopold further describes the relationship of the individual element with other elements of that system, and he identifies the kind of community that such relationships create: "A thing is right when it tends to preserve the integrity, stability, and beauty of the biotic community."[7] (This is certainly a splendid definition of *catholicity*.)

In a similar vein, in the 1970s chemist James Lovelock developed the Gaia Hypothesis, named Gaia after the Greek goddess of Earth. This theory claims that all organisms along with

[6] Aldo Leopold, *A Sand County Almanac: And Sketches Here and There* (New York: Oxford University Press, 1949), 243.

[7] Ibid., 262.

their inorganic environment are so interrelated that a single self-regulating complex system is formed that maintains life on Earth. Those who espouse this view argue that Earth itself in its totality is a living creation, functioning according to a myriad of interrelated systems.[8] This hypothesis was co-developed by Lynn Margulis, a microbiologist whose own theory of endosymbiosis is now considered scientific orthodoxy. Though some of the aspects of the Gaia Hypothesis have generated controversy in the scientific world, its fundamental premise remains intact, namely, that some form of symbiotic relationship exists within and among all of Earth's creatures. This insight leads one to conclude that human beings do not merely live on Earth but are in fact a form of living Earth. (Another insight into our fundamental catholicity.)

A sense of the interconnectedness of Earth creatures is reflected in the biblical tradition as well. In the second creation narrative we read that God formed the first human Earth creature from the ground (Gen 2:7). Later in that same narrative God made the trees (v. 9) and the animals (v. 19) out of the same ground. This community of Earth is also evident in the account of the covenant that God initiated after the flood. That covenant was made with Noah and his descendants, indicating its intergenerational character. However, it was also made with every living creature on Earth:

> "As for me, I am establishing my covenant with you and your descendants after you, and with every living creature that is with you, the birds, the domestic animals, and every animal of the earth with you, as many as came out of the ark." (Gen 9:9–10)

and with Earth itself:

> "I have set my bow in the clouds, and it shall be a sign of the covenant between me and the earth." (Gen 9:13)

---

[8] In line with this perspective *Earth* in this book refers to the entire self-regulating complex system.

Furthermore, the fourth commandment of the Decalogue as found in Deuteronomy states that animals are to be included in the Sabbath rest from work:

> But the seventh day is a sabbath to the LORD your God; you shall not do any work—you, or your son or your daughter, or your male or female slave, or your ox or your donkey, or any of your livestock, or the resident alien in your towns, so that your male and female slave may rest as well as you. (Deut 5:14)

And the Book of Leviticus prescribes that every seventh year even the land should lie fallow and enjoy Sabbath rest:

> The seventh year there shall be a sabbath of complete rest for the land, a sabbath for the LORD: you shall not sow your field or prune your vineyard. (Lev 25:4)

This connectedness of all natural creation is found in other passages of the Old Testament, suggesting that the theme was not limited to one or two periods of Israelite history, nor was it an exceptional point of view. Rather, the sense of connectedness with Earth appears to have been quite common in ancient Israel's thinking.

This web of life has long been recognized and celebrated by indigenous people around the world. A prayer of the Lakota Sioux of the Great Plains of the United States, "Mitakuye Oyasin—For All My Relatives," expresses oneness and harmony with all forms of life. This includes other people, animals, birds, insects, trees and plants, and even rocks, rivers, mountains, and valleys. We need not go outside our religious tradition to find insight into our membership with all of creation. In his "Canticle of the Sun," Francis of Assisi celebrates members of natural creation as his sisters or brothers. We fail to grasp the depth of this point of view if we dismiss it as simply an artistic metaphor devised by a simple though creative mind.

These examples of insight into the interconnectedness of Earth and all Earth creatures do not suggest that earlier people of various cultures enjoyed the sophisticated scientific knowledge that we have come to today. Rather, lacking the control that scientific understanding often provides, their immediate experience of life forces enabled them to recognize their dependence on those forces and their interdependence with other Earth creatures. Our current ability to control many of these forces may have dulled our sense of dependence upon them.

Overview of the Book

The Bible is a collection of religious testimonies that originated at different times in history and were later compiled in a way that advanced certain important religious themes such as deliverance, divine election, covenant, messianism, and so on. These testimonies have come down to us in various literary forms, including myth, law, prophecy, proverb, gospel, epistle, and apocalyptic. The present study chooses passages from various sections of the Bible in which an aspect of natural creation plays a significant role, and it examines those passages using the lens of community of Earth. Some of the passages will be well known to the reader. Others might be unfamiliar.

Chapter 1 looks at the Pentateuch (Genesis, Exodus, Leviticus, Numbers, and Deuteronomy), in which the ancestors' movements from water source to water source can be tracked. An examination of passages in which water plays a prominent role fits naturally into the focus of this study. The ancient Israelites' various attitudes toward the land in which they settled is a major theme in the Historical Books (Joshua, Judges, 1 and 2 Samuel, 1 and 2 Kings). This is addressed in Chapter 2. Many prophets rose up at moments of crisis throughout Israel's history. Chapter 3 examines the messages of Amos and Hosea, two prophets in the north who critiqued Israel's failure to deal with the land as required by the covenant made with God. The order within the natural world is the subject of much of the Wisdom tradition (Proverbs, Job, Qoheleth, Wisdom of Solomon, and Sirach). Facets of ancient Israelite cosmological thinking found in the Wisdom tradition are discussed in Chapter 4. The Gospels present four different portrayals of Jesus. Chapter 5 uncovers the cosmological underpinnings of some of the nature imagery found in the Gospels. Paul is passionate about the new creation that resulted from the resurrection of Jesus. Chapter 6 looks at passages where this is found. Finally, the theme of a new heaven and new earth as found in Revelation is the subject of Chapter 7.

"A wandering Aramean was my ancestor"

—Deuteronomy 26:5b

Chapter One

The history of a people not only contains stories of their past, but also the basis of their present identity. These stories need not be historically accurate in every detail, but the important ones capture the essence of some aspect of the people's character, and to that extent they are reliable. This is true about stories in the Old Testament as well. They tell us how the ancient Israelites understood themselves, their place in the world, and their relationship with the divine.

For both the ancient Israelites and the contemporary Jewish community the heart of their religious tradition and the basis of their identity are found in the first five books of the Bible, which they call Torah or Law and Christians call the Pentateuch ("five books"). Here we read that out of all the people in the world, God chose their ancestor to be the progenitor of a nation that would be special to God. This people entered into a covenant with God, who promised them land and protection and required that they live according to God's design. However, before they could settle in this promised land, generation after generation of them moved from place to place. The stories in this first section of the Bible contain the fundamental tenets of Israelite faith: they were chosen by God to be God's special people; because of the covenant God initiated with them, they committed themselves to a specific manner of living; though they were promised a specific land, they never forgot that they were originally wanderers.

Major figures explode on the scene in this first section of the Bible. We are well acquainted with men such as Abraham, Isaac, Jacob, Joseph, and Moses. Feminists remind us of the importance of women like Sarah and Hagar, Rebekah, Rachel and Leah, and Miriam. However, other people played significant roles in this history, though they have not always been valued, people like Esau and Abimelech. Passing quickly over references to women or non-Israelite individuals is evidence of the gender or ethnic bias in the stories. This book seeks to uncover another pervasive bias, namely, anthropocentrism, or perceiving humans as the center or goal of everything. This first chapter looks anew at stories that depict the often overlooked indispensability of water in the land through which these ancient people moved.

Literary Context

The accounts in the Torah or Pentateuch trace the movements of this people from their original home in Mesopotamia, west across the top of the Arabian Peninsula to the land of Canaan, south into the Negev desert, down into Egypt, and finally north again to the eastern shore of the Jordan River. The movements followed well-established caravan and trade routes, routes that track various sources of water. The journey itself began at one river, the Euphrates, and ended at another, the Jordan. The people would not have been able to move in the direction they took had there not been sources of indispensable water.

Most scholars today agree that, while these accounts are narrative in form, they are not to be understood as literal history. Innovative literary forms such as metaphor, hyperbole, and myth were used to express the people's understanding of the events of their life. Furthermore, these are testimonies of faith, reports of how over a long period of time the people perceived God active in their lives. Consequently, it is necessary to understand not only what is being reported, but also the theological meaning of that report. This in no way negates the importance of the historical dimension of these testimonies, for it was within the context of the people's actual life that they experienced God. The social, political, and religious context of that life has been the subject of much scholarship. But only recently have the ecological implications of these contexts become the subject of serious study. The present work sees itself as part of this latter venture. It examines selected biblical passages from the perspective of the community of Earth in order to situate humankind within this community as a part of it and dependent on it for survival and enrichment rather than aloof from it and disdainful of it.

The earliest ancestors of Israel were probably herders who followed their flocks from one fertile pasturage to another (Gen 13:2). As wanderers, these people were aliens in the lands of other tribes and, consequently, dependent on the hospitality of those tribes. Such hospitality was universally extended by desert communities, because without it survival during travel was tenuous at best. Egyptian archaeological findings describe several important movements of people from the east. The ancestors of ancient Israel were probably included among these people. The major role in this migratory drama played by sources of water should not be underestimated. These water sources probably determined the direction taken by the people and the length of the sojourn spent at various sites. The Bible reports that after several generations of moving around in Canaan, famine caused by drought brought these early travelers to Egypt, where they not only survived but eventually flourished (Gen 47:1–12).

When a new pharaoh rose to power in Egypt, the political tides turned against these Asiatic people, and they found themselves at the mercy of oppressors (Exod 1:8–10). According to the Bible, the mighty waters of Egypt, which had always been life sustaining for the Egyptians, became a source of salvation for the ancestors of Israel as well. The story of their deliverance begins with a report of an infant boy saved from extinction by the Egyptians when he was hidden in the reeds of the Nile River. He was rescued by Pharaoh's daughter and raised as her son. Years later this same boy, now grown and known as Moses, reclaimed his original identity and led his people out of Egyptian oppression. The story describes how, once again, Egyptian waters played an important role in the deliverance of this people as they passed through the "Sea of Reeds" (Exod 14:26–29). The exact place of their passage is unknown, but it was probably part of the narrow strip of water between Egypt in northern Africa and the Arabian peninsula to the east. Traditionally, this strip of water has been known as the Red Sea.

After crossing the Sea of Reeds, the people faced the rigors of existence in an arid wasteland. In this wilderness they faced the possibility of life-threatening thirst. The biblical story relates how they were rescued from this adversity (Exod 17:6; Num 20:11). They would never have survived this trek across the ancient Near East had they not found water along the way. Nor would they have been able to carry on in a foreign land had not the inhabitants of that land shared their own sources of water with them. Once again we see the people's complete dependence on water.

In reading such stories we too frequently concentrate solely on human struggles and human feats without taking into account the fundamental need for water that lays bare the people's total dependence on components of Earth. This need has never been denied. However, the relationship between humankind and the rest of the natural world has usually been seen as one of utility and exploitation rather than connectedness, interdependence, and oneness. The community of Earth perspective calls for a major shift in anthropological understanding. This might also require a fresh reading of biblical passages that have been used to reinforce anthropocentricism. In line with this, what follows is a closer look at sections of this first part of Israel's story with an eye to the pivotal role that water plays in these accounts. This reading concentrates on stories that feature or mention rivers, springs, or wells.

Life-Giving Water

Water is life. As we all know, water is the most abundant component of Earth. One might say that it is Earth's life force, because it is essential for the survival of all of Earth's living creatures. This includes humans, animals, and vegetation. Though the human body appears to be solid substance, more than two-thirds of it is water; the human brain is 95 percent water; and human blood is 82 percent water. Therefore, it is fair to say that not only is water life giving and sustaining, but in human beings water itself is actually living. It is no wonder that, in many cultures, water has come to have religious importance. In fact, various forms of water have even been considered divine.

The physical world in which the ancestors of Israel lived shaped their world of understanding. The abundance or scarcity of water influenced their manner of living and the way they perceived God's action in their lives. While unruly water appears occasionally in several biblical passages in the first five books of the Bible under consideration here, as well as in Psalms—for example, "You rule the raging sea; you still its swelling waves" (Ps 89:10)—water is usually depicted as peaceful and refreshing, a necessary component of life.

The climate of the land of Canaan, the land in which the people eventually settled, led them to appreciate the importance of water. This land is semi-tropical, with two major seasons, the dry season from May or June through September and the wet season from mid-October or November through March. Usually no rain at all falls during the dry season, while during the wet season, most of the rainfall occurs between November and February. The early rain in autumn softens the ground, making it pliable for plowing and sowing. The heavy winter rain soaks the ground and, because water is at such a premium, the overflow is captured and retained in cisterns for later use. The late spring rain fosters crop growth. Westerly winds that blow off the Mediterranean Sea are moist, while the easterly winds that blow from the desert bring the burning khamsin or sirocco winds. Rain decreases from the west to the east and from the north to the south. Rainfall in the uplands, though not always abundant, is generally sufficient for agriculture and herding, depending upon the winds.[1] This explains why sources of water like rivers, springs, and wells were so important for the people of biblical times who lived in these lands.[2]

Rivers

Geography is important to this study, not merely because it charts land formation, climate, and life forms, but because it also

---

[1] Philip J. King and Lawrence E. Stager, *Life in Biblical Israel* (Louisville, KY: Westminster John Knox, 2001), 122–28.

[2] Laura Hobgood-Oster, "'For Out of That Well the Flocks Were Watered': Stories of Wells in Genesis," in *The Earth Bible*, vol. 2, *The Earth Story in Genesis*, ed. Norman C. Habel and Shirley Wurst (Sheffield, UK: Sheffield Academic Press, 2000), 187–99.

explains how human beings understand themselves in relation to their environment. The environment largely determines the occupations that enable the people to survive and thrive there. It also influences the character of cultural realities such as food, clothing, and shelter, as well as various social and moral standards and values such as sharing and protecting. Geography also inspires the ways people understand God. For example, the characterization of God as a good shepherd is most likely to originate from people who live off the land, rather than from mariners.

Much of the history of ancient Israel unfolded on the banks of four major rivers: the Tigris, the Euphrates, the Nile, and the Jordan. While these rivers acted externally as geographic and political boundaries, they also influenced the shape of the people's internal geography or world of understanding. Three of these rivers, the Tigris, the Euphrates in Mesopotamia, and the Nile in Egypt, are geographic points on a series of water sources that flow from Western Asia, west over the top of the Arabian Peninsula, then south into Northern Africa. The ancestors of Israel followed this arc of waterways, known as the Fertile Crescent, and settled in Canaan, which was located in the western part of the arc. The fourth river, the Jordan, flows from north of the Sea of Galilee in Canaan south into the Dead Sea. This river was the scene of several important events in the history of Israel.

The exact city of origin of Israel's ancestors is unclear, because biblical names sometimes refer to places and at other times the same name identifies a person. Most commentators maintain that the ancestors came from Ur of the Chaldeans (Gen 11:28, 31), a major city in ancient Mesopotamia. Mesopotamia is a geographic designation, not a political one. The word comes from the Greek, meaning "between the rivers." It is the land between the Tigris on the east and the Euphrates on the west. Many of the greatest Ancient Near Eastern civilizations grew out of this very fertile region. The respective civilization often took the name of its major city, for example, Sumerian from Sumer; Akkadian from Akkad; Assyria from Asshur; Babylonian from Babel. Ur itself was located on the western bank of the Euphrates. It was known as a center of international trade as well as scribal and religious activity. Thus the ancestors of the Israelites came from a highly civilized part of the ancient world.

The first move made by this family was north to Haran (Gen 11:31), an important center of religious and political activity. Like Ur, the major god at Haran was a lunar deity. This ancient religious belief might explain why the Israelites marked the beginning of the day at sunset, when the moon begins to rule the heavens ("And there was evening and there was morning, the first day" [Gen 1:5]). Ur's destruction by an invading army could account for the people's move to Haran. It was at Haran that Abram was told to migrate across the Fertile Crescent, following the water routes to the land of Canaan (Gen 12:1). It is not clear whether Canaan or Egypt was his intended destination, for he and his company traveled as far south as the Negev desert (Gen 12:9). This entire journey would have been an extremely difficult feat to undertake if these people had been agriculturalists, for farming requires a significant block of time to prepare the land and then more time for planting, growing, and harvesting. As already stated, the biblical stories depict Abram and his people as herders, moving from oasis to oasis following their flocks and herds in search of water and the vegetation that grows near such water sources.

The Tigris and Euphrates also influenced the religious imagination of the Israelites, shaping their understanding of creation. The confluence of the waters of these two mighty rivers often resulted in flooding. This was not a regular and gradual flooding, as was experienced in Egypt with the Nile. Rather, it was often a violent flooding that resulted in destruction and loss of life, as recounted in various flood narratives (see Gen 7—8). Most likely these unruly waters are reflected in the Enuma Elish, the Babylonian account of creation. That story reports how the god of fresh water married the god of salty ocean water. This union of waters caused great turmoil that disturbed the other gods. Angry at such disruption, those gods sent a young warrior deity, Marduk, to quell the chaos. A great cosmic battle ensued. Marduk conquered the unruly waters by killing the ferocious water deity Tiamat. He then cut her in half horizontally. Out of the upper half of her carcass he fashioned the heavens, while the lower part became Earth. This battle and the establishment of order was reenacted yearly in Babylon as part of the New Year celebration.

Though water does not play a comparable role in Israel's creation narratives, traces of this myth remain in its creation narrative in the description of the construction of the dome and the separation of waters:

> So God made the dome and separated the waters that were under the dome from the waters that were above the dome. (Gen 1:7)

Whether this earlier influence left its mark on Israel's ancestors when the people originally lived in Ur and Haran, or much later at the time of the people's exile in Babylon (587 BCE) is not clear. What is clear is the influence that the Sumerian environment played in shaping the worldview of the people living in that area, which included the ancestors of Israel.

In yet another Genesis account a river coursed out of the garden in Eden, dividing into four main branches that flowed into the four corners of Earth. The branches are the Pishon, the Gihon, the Tigris, and the Euphrates (Gen 2:10–14). These branches represent the four major rivers of the world known by the Israelites. The Tigris and the Euphrates define the borders of Mesopotamia in Asia; the Pishon is thought to have been some place in Arabia; and the Gihon is in modern-day Ethiopia. Although there is no place on Earth where these four rivers converge, the reference in the creation account is meant to present this garden as the source of life and fertility for the entire world.

Even after Abram's migration out of the Euphrates Valley, the river continued to play an important role in the ongoing story of that people. When God sealed with a covenant the promise of land made with Abram, the scope of the land promised extended "from the river of Egypt to the great river, the river Euphrates" (Gen 15:18), an area that encompassed most of the Fertile Crescent. This promise was reiterated to Abram's descendants after they had escaped from Egyptian bondage:

> "I will set your borders from the Red Sea to the sea of the Philistines, and from the wilderness to the Euphrates." (Exod 23:31)

> "Every place on which you set foot shall be yours; your territory shall extend from the wilderness to the Lebanon

and from the River Euphrates, to the Western Sea." (Deut 11:24)

Many commentators believe that these wide-ranging boundaries reflect the dreams of expansion that originated during the time of the monarchy rather than identify territory that was ever really controlled by the Israelite kings. Despite the origin of the tradition, interpretation of this promise of land and the realization of the boundaries sketched in it have been at the heart of contested land claims in Israel/Palestine down through the centuries, even to this day.

Finally, the very designation *Hebrew* means "across" or "beyond." Abram was first called a Hebrew in Genesis 14:13. It is interesting to note that in the Bible this term was only used by non-Israelites or when Israelites were talking to foreigners. The designation indicates that the Israelites were regarded as outsiders, as people from across the river, presumably the Euphrates River. The Tigris does not seem to have carried the same importance in the early traditions of the Israelites as did the Euphrates. However, it reappears much later in Israel's account of the conversion of Nineveh, the city that was built on the banks of that river (see the Book of Jonah).

While the origins of the Israelite people can be traced back to Mesopotamia, the land between the Tigris and the Euphrates, it was the waterways of Egypt that were prominent in the shaping of their national identity. The people living in Canaan were dependent on springs and rainfall for the water needed for both herding and any subsistence farming in which they were involved. This meant that any serious depletion of these water sources could result in drought and subsequent famine. Egypt, on the other hand, enjoyed an entirely different life along the banks of the Nile. That river floods annually in the spring, depositing extremely fertile soil as its waters recede. In ancient times irrigation canals captured the overflow of this flooding, directing the water throughout the vicinity and expanding the extent of arable land. In this way the Egyptians were able to produce an abundance of necessary food crops.

Israel's ancestors living in drought-ridden Canaan often faced the hardship of famine and were driven to seek temporary refuge elsewhere. Accounts of such situations are found throughout the early stories of the Bible:

> Now there was a famine in the land. So Abram went down to Egypt to reside there as an alien, for the famine was severe in the land. (Gen 12:10)

> Now there was a famine in the land, besides the former famine that had occurred in the days of Abraham. And Isaac went to Gerar, to King Abimelech of the Philistines. (Gen 26:1)

Another story describes the harsh and extensive famine that brought Jacob, his sons, and their families to Egypt, where they settled for an extended period of time:

> Thus the sons of Israel were among the other people who came to buy grain, for the famine had reached the land of Canaan. (Gen 42:5)

> You shall settle in the land of Goshen, and you shall be near me, you and your children and your children's children, as well as your flocks, your herds and all that you have. (Gen 45:10)

Goshen was a fertile region in the eastern part of the Nile delta. It was well suited for grazing. Though few of the stories of Israel's ancestors can be corroborated by sources outside the Bible, mention of a settlement such as the one in Goshen is found in Egyptian records. The allusion there to Asiatic migrants living in the northeastern part of the delta could be a reference to the family of Jacob.

The story of the ancestors in Egypt continues:

> Now a new king arose over Egypt, who did not know Joseph. He said to his people, "Look, the Israelite people are more numerous and more powerful than we." (Exod 1:8–9)

In an attempt to resolve this situation, the king decided upon the slaughter of newborn Hebrew boys. However, the Hebrew midwives Shiphrah and Puah could not bring themselves to obey this appalling order, and so the infants were saved. Nonetheless, a second order was issued:

> "Every boy that is born to the Hebrews you shall throw into the Nile." (Exod 1:22)

The Egyptian river that had been the source of life and prosperity for Jacob and his family was now to become the burial site of his descendants. This disastrous situation set the stage for the story of the rescue of Moses. Placed in a papyrus basket that was reinforced with bitumen and pitch, he was positioned among the reeds on the bank of the Nile. The pharaoh's daughter found him there and, though she knew he was a Hebrew baby, she brought him into her home and raised him as her own son. Once again the Nile protected the future of this people.

Certainly the most dramatic biblical episode involving the Nile is the complex account of the Hebrews' dramatic escape from Egyptian servitude (Exod 7—11). Whether their release from bondage was considered a remedy for the discrimination the Israelites suffered at the hands of the Egyptians or a call to worship in the wilderness, the insistence of God and the reluctance of Pharaoh set the stage for a series of contests known as the plagues.

Various interpretations of these plagues have been advanced. Some commentators argue that the plagues were a chain of natural phenomena brought on by changes in climate and environment. The first plague, the Nile turned into blood (Exod 7:20), could have been the result of rising temperatures that caused the river to move slowly and thus allowed the growth of a kind of algae that turned water red. This condition would kill the fish and cause the frogs to escape the water for land—the second plague (8:2). Frogs do not survive well outside water; when they died, the gnats and insects that they would normally have eaten would be free to infest the land—the third and fourth plagues (8:13, 20). Gnats and flies often transmit disease to livestock and human beings alike—the fifth and sixth plagues (9:6, 10). When the river water no longer enlivens the surrounding land, drought can cause locusts in search of food to swarm—the eighth plague (10:14). Darkness, the ninth plague (10:22), could result from the huge swarms of locusts or from a sudden summer storm accompanied by devastating hail—the seventh plague (9:23). All this natural devastation could certainly result in the death of children, because they are some of the most vulnerable individuals in the society—the tenth plague (12:29).

The Bible presents these disasters as contests between the power of the God of Israel and that of the Egyptian magicians, meant to demonstrate the matchless might and all-encompassing dominance of the God of Israel. People of the ancient world believed that gods only exercised power within the territory of their own people. Thus, the gods of Egypt would be expected to prevail over the God of Israel. However, the opposite came about. According to this point of view, the God of Israel not only wielded power in this foreign land but even demonstrated power over nature, far surpassing the power of the Egyptian gods.

The plagues may well reflect actual climate and environmental disasters that have at times beset the Nile floodplain and delta area. Such demythologization in no way denies the action of God. It merely rejects the idea of direct action on the part of God, not indirect action through the design and forces of the natural world. This complex of natural occurrences could be an example of the interconnectedness of components of Earth. It should be noted that the stories tell how the Egyptians suffered from these disasters, while the Israelites were preserved from them. If there is a miraculous event, it lies in this distinction. The entire tradition of the plagues could simply be an exaggerated detail of an ancient saga meant to emphasize God's protection of this vulnerable people.

Springs

Springs are marvelous works of nature. They arise from some mysterious source deep within Earth. Because these waters move among underground rocks, they are both purified and enriched by minerals that are dissolved in them. This explains the beneficial character of spring water. Their flowing nature has led some to refer to them as "living water." Sometimes the spring acts like a fountain, welling up to the surface of Earth of its own accord and its waters become available to quench the thirst of humans, animals, and Earth itself.

Stories that feature springs often report that a momentous event occurred near the spring, and the mysterious character of that event caused the spring to be revered as sacred. Many believe that the spring is memorable because of its effect on human beings, thus valuing it merely for its instrumental importance. Actually, the reverse is probably true; the spring has value in itself. Its life-giving character is an aspect of its intrinsic power, a power that is present whether or not human beings are sustained by it. The spring does not achieve value merely through human agency, as an anthropocentric perspective might claim. Rather, its mere existence as a member of the community of Earth is the basis of its value. Its ability to sustain and nurture life flows from this and exemplifies the interconnectedness of Earth's living creatures as well as human beings' complete dependence on it.

Several stories featuring springs include reports of hardships the people had to overcome as they moved from place to place. These stories are found in the collection of narratives describing their journeying in the wilderness after the deliverance from bondage in Egypt. Traditionally, these hardships have been understood as tests that seek to discover whether or not the people trusted in God's care. Such an interpretation casts God in a somewhat negative light. One might ask why a caring God would treat a vulnerable people in such a harsh manner. Ancient people might well have considered these hardships as obstacles placed in their path by capricious gods, but contemporary readers might understand this in a very different way. Having a more scientific grasp of the design and forces of nature, and reading from the perspective of the world in front of the text, they understand the meaning of these passages another way.

The people's desperate need of water is the issue in two of these stories. The first one (Exod 15:22–25a) does not explicitly state that the water came from a spring. However, the water source does not appear to have been a well. The people had only recently been safely brought by Moses through the Sea of Reeds into this wilderness. After traveling three days, they finally came upon water, but it was bitter to the taste. This place was called Marah, which means "bitterness," an appropriate name for such water. The people complained about their plight. In response to their murmuring, God directed Moses to throw a piece of wood into the water, and the bitter water became sweet to the taste.

Contrary to what some commentators have claimed, there is no indication that this was a test of the loyalty of the people. Nor does the text indicate that this reversal in the nature of the water was a miracle. A scientifically unsophisticated view might make such a judgment. However, contemporary acquired knowledge of the properties of some species of trees suggests that the wood might have effected the change. Therefore, rather than a test of loyalty, this story might exemplify the interconnectedness of the components of Earth, namely, humans' need for water and wood's ability to change the character of that water. The disconnect between the name Marah, which describes the initial condition of the water, and the water's final sweet character can serve as a sign and a reminder that the gracious creator does indeed work in the lives of people, though indirectly, through the mysterious powers of nature.

The water at Elim, the next stop on the journey, was clearly a spring (Exod 15:27; Num 33:9). In fact, this site had twelve springs. It must have been a sizable oasis, the kind of setting that could have inspired the description of the garden in Eden (see Gen 2:10–14). No memorable event occurred here; no name is given.

Further into the wilderness trek, a second hardship involving water took place (Exod 17:1–7; Num 20:2–11). As was the case earlier, the people complained of thirst. It should be noted that they questioned Moses's leadership, accusing him of bringing them into a waterless wilderness to die. (In the Numbers version Aaron is accused as well.) Once again, in response to their murmuring, God intervened and provided the water that they needed to survive. The staff used by Moses to part the Sea of Reeds and enable the Israelites to cross over on the dry seabed (Exod 14:6) was now used to strike a rock, causing water to gush forth. Once again, some contemporary commentators claim that God was testing their loyalty. The text does not say this. On the contrary, it is Moses who claimed that their questioning of his leadership constituted a test by them of God's providential care. Thus, it is God's providential care itself that is tested, not the people's confidence in that care.

Contrary to traditional interpretation, there is no indication in the text that this event was a miracle, though the people unfamiliar with the wilderness within which they found themselves might have seen it as such. Some commentators suggest that the rock was actually an aquifer in the wilderness. They hold that striking it in just the right way might have produced a flow of water. To question the possible miraculous nature of this event is not to deny divine power. Instead, it suggests, as seen above, that it is precisely through the delicate and intricate forces of nature that the creator works in the lives of the people.[3] This underscores again the connectedness and interdependence of components of Earth. It demonstrates how ecosystems created by God support all of the members of that system.

The place where this second event occurred has two names. The first name, Massah, means "despair" and points to the despondency of the people in the absence of the water they so desperately needed. The second name, Meribah, means "strife" or "contention." It describes the people's attitude toward Moses, who led them into this waterless place. The disparaging names of this site, which has become a source of life-giving water, are reminders of the negative attitudes of the fickle people, not of the water itself. As with the account of the waters of Marah, there is a disconnect between the life-sustaining character of the water and its disparaging name, a disconnect that points to human limitation when facing a new and challenging environment, not to any quality of the water itself.

The idea that God tested the people in the wilderness when they were most vulnerable is very troubling for many today. It reinforces the idea that natural disasters like earthquakes, hurricanes, and tsunamis are punishments for human sinfulness. The thirst the people experienced in this unfamiliar and inhospitable terrain was clearly a hardship, but it was not a punishment. It was a natural effect of the geographic location in which they

---

[3] This is in line with a characteristic of divine action. Denis Edwards writes: "God's action is not interventionist, but works consistently in and through the laws of nature, rather than by violating or bypassing them." See "Exploring How God Acts," in *God, Grace, and Creation*, College Theology Society Annual 55, ed. Philip J. Rossi (Maryknoll, NY: Orbis Books, 2010), 127.

found themselves. But was it a test, as many commentators argue? The hermeneutic of suspicion leads one to ask: Might one say that, if it was a test, it was the unfamiliar environment that tested the people's ability to adapt? These wilderness stories of water scarcity underscore the total dependence of human beings on water. They also suggest that the hardships in the wilderness challenged the people to discover ways of existing in a new environment. As we know today, such a challenge of adaptability is a fundamental characteristic of the cosmic design of our constantly evolving universe. Only that which can adapt to changing circumstances will survive.

Insight into this aspect of the world of which we are a part throws an entirely different light on the nature of the hardships and challenges that we all face. They are not punishments that can be avoided by conformity to a set of social or religious mandates, much less pointless obstacles thrown in our path by an unpredictable deity. They are often natural occurrences that emerge from the complexity and randomness of life itself. The way we deal with them lays bare the measure of our adaptability and the character of our moral fiber.

Once again, such demythologizing in no way disputes the power of the creator. Rather, it maintains that this divine power works through the design and forces of nature, not against or outside of them. Understanding divine activity in this way also sketches a very different anthropological profile. Being spurred on to discover traces of nature's design and some of its hidden forces calls forth human ingenuity. It also enables human beings to advance in understanding and living within the community of Earth.

Wells

Springs are marvels of nature itself, while wells are artificial shafts burrowed into Earth in order to tap the water table or to capture underground spring water. Wells might mark the site of momentous events, but the events occur where they do because there is first a spring present. The spring is essential for the survival of living forms, and the well is an inventive human means of providing access to the water.

It is important to remember that the stories about Israel's very earliest ancestors are clothed in the cultural garb common to traditional societies. An initial look at these customs will help clarify aspects of the story. Israel was patriarchal (*pater*, father; *arche*, head) in its political and social organization and androcentric (*andró*, male; *kéntro*, centric) in its point of view. In such societies it is the men who make the major decisions, choosing what is important for the entire group. In several accounts found in the Pentateuch the ancestors are portrayed as specially chosen by God from among all other peoples and nations. Thus, we should not be surprised to find both gender and ethnic or social biases in the stories they tell about themselves. Such biases play a very important role in the next story considered.

Sarai, Abram's wife, was unable to conceive and bear him an heir (Gen 16). According to the existing social laws, a barren wife could engage a surrogate to bear a child in her place. This infant would then be adopted by the barren woman, be considered her child, and if a boy, could become the legal heir of the husband. Sarai had such a slave-girl, an Egyptian named Hagar, and she gave Hagar to Abram as a concubine or secondary wife. Hagar was fertile, and when she conceived, she treated the barren Sarai with disdain. In retaliation, Sarai abused the foreign Hagar so badly that she ran away. In the scene under consideration, "The angel of the LORD found [Hagar] by a spring of water in the wilderness, the spring on the way to Shur" (Gen 16:7).

Several aspects of this story are unusual. First, visitation by a heavenly being was usually granted to men, not to women. Second, the heavenly visitor came to a foreigner, an Egyptian, someone who may have worshiped Egyptian gods. Third, this Egyptian was a slave, perhaps part of the spoils of some war. Having fled her mistress, she was now also a fugitive. This unusual event transpired at a spring. It is important to note that this source of water was open to all, even one whose very existence denoted separation and alienation: a woman, a foreigner, a fugitive slave.

None of these cultural barriers prevented Hagar access to the water. Her fundamental right as an Earth creature intimately connected with and dependent upon water cut through gender, ethnic, class, and religious biases, biases that often separated groups of people from one another. This aspect of universality or catholicity should not be overlooked. It is evidence that divine providential care embraces all, regardless of authentic cultural distinctions that might exist. Furthermore, the visitation of the heavenly being, with its promise of blessing rather than condemnation for unacceptable behavior, confirmed Hagar's right to this water. It is clear from these details that in this ancient culture water was not the exclusive property of some at the expense of others. Access to water was a universal right.

Recognizing the extraordinary character of this experience, Hagar named both the heavenly visitor and the well where the visitation took place:

> "You are El-roi"; for she said, "Have I really seen God and remained alive after seeing him?" Therefore the well was called Beer-lahai-roi. (Gen 16:13–14)

Though the Hebrew in this passage is difficult to translate, most commentators maintain that El-Roi means "God-seeing" and Beer-lahai-roi means "Well of the living one who sees." Just what was seen? Hagar claims to have seen God (the angel represents divine self-disclosure), but the well is named for God who sees, not for a vision of the divine. What did God see? God certainly saw Hagar's oppression by Sarai, for the heavenly messenger directed her: "Return to your mistress, and submit to her" (Gen 16:9). God sees this particular oppression, just as in the future God will "see" the oppression suffered under Egyptian bondage (Exod 3:9–10). When used of God, the Hebrew verb meaning "to see" means "to see a need and to address it." God sees Hagar's subjugation, and though she is directed to return to subjugation, a remarkable promise is made. Not only will she survive, but a hardy desert people will spring from her. At this life-giving water her life is saved as is the mighty nation that is growing within her womb.

Some readers might be distressed that Hagar is told to return to subjugation. However, the fact that this foreign woman, who was a fugitive slave, not only had free access to the water but was also the recipient of a divine visitation and told that her unborn child would be the founder of a great people demonstrates that the power of God is not constrained by human biases even though the biases remain in society.

The well was on a caravan route to Shur in the Sinai Peninsula. Though Hagar's experience was probably private, the well itself was a public stopping place for travelers. Thus, as a source of needed water, it was already recognized as a site where life was renewed. In the future all those who would come to this spring for water would revere the place as a sacred site, for a messenger from heaven confirmed the right of one whose cultural reality marked her as marginal to have access to the indispensable water.

Wells are indispensable for nomadic herders like Israel's earliest ancestors. Since caravan routes through the wilderness are usually established near wells, those who oversee them benefit from the service offered and any exchange of goods that might take place there. Frequently conflicts arose over the water rights of the wells. One such conflict involved Abraham and Abimelech the king of Gerar (Gen 21:25–32). Abimelech gave Abraham flocks and herds and free access to some of his own land (Gen 20:15). However, Abraham later alleged that Abimelech's servants forcibly seized a well on that very land. The king claimed lack of knowledge of such aggressive behavior. Somewhat suspicious of the circumstances surrounding this action, Abraham sought a way of reconciling the tension between the two groups of people. He offered Abimelech sheep, cattle, and seven ewe lambs, and then initiated a covenant with him. (A covenant is a legal agreement between two parties that entails obligations on both sides.) Not all such agreements were sealed with a covenant. The seriousness of this particular agreement signifies the importance of this well.

Abraham's transaction resulted in and guaranteed future peaceful relations. A gift consisting of ewe lambs was most unusual. Their potential for breeding and producing milk makes female animals much more valuable than the male members of the species. One does not normally relinquish such valuable animals. The fact that these sheep were lambs adds to their value, because of their long future of productivity. Abraham presents Abimelech a most valuable gift, one that the king could not refuse without insulting the giver. The quality of the gift highlights again the importance Abraham placed on control of this well.

The site where this transaction took place was called Beersheba, which means "well of seven." Just as in an earlier story where the well named Beer-lahai-roi reminded people of the promise God made to Hagar (16:14), so Beer-sheba would remind them of the importance of this well and of the covenant that gave people access to it despite their competition. In both instances the sites continued to enjoy great significance because their life-giving waters symbolized life itself—life for Hagar and her child in the first story, and life for the two parties that initially quarreled over use of the well in this second account.

A similar account of the resolution of strife is found in the cycle of stories that feature Abraham's son Isaac. Famine in the land drove Isaac from the area near Beer-lahai-roi where he and his family were living (Gen 25:11), and they traveled south to the land of Gerar. There Isaac reopened some of the wells that had been dug earlier by Abraham's men. There seems to have been no problem with his doing this. However, when Isaac's shepherds dug a new well and found spring water, they were challenged by the shepherds of Gerar, who claimed: "The water is ours" (Gen 25:20). This well was then called Esek, which comes from the Hebrew verb meaning "to quarrel." A second well was dug; a similar dispute took place; and this second well was called Sitnah, which is derived from the verb meaning "to be an adversary." A third well was dug, but for reasons not mentioned, no quarrel resulted over this well. This well was then called Rehoboth, which comes from the verb meaning "to be wide," implying that there was room enough at this well for all of the contenders. Such stories underscore the desperate need living creatures have for water. Furthermore, they must devise ways that they can avail themselves of this water and also allow other living creatures to do the same. Once again, dependence on water demonstrates interconnectedness of Earth creatures and the need for patterns of social interrelatedness within an ecosystem.

Perhaps the most interesting stories describing events that occur at wells are reports of the search for wives for the ancestors. In a patriarchal society like ancient Israel, the importance of finding the right wife for the heir of the household cannot be overemphasized. This is one of the patriarch's most serious responsibilities, for the future of the household depends upon it. In such societies marriage is usually arranged by the chief men in the respective families. The union is understood primarily as a legal agreement between families, and only secondarily as an emotional attachment between the individuals involved.

There are basically two kinds of marriage, exogamous and endogamous (*exo*—marrying outside of one's tribe or clan; *endo*—marrying within). Exogamous marriage is meant to establish ties between various groups and to foster enriching cultural exchange. It is usually practiced by groups that enjoy a strong sense of identity, one that is not threatened by the diversity and change that result from interacting with people of a different group. An endogamous marriage is meant to ensure the purity of the male bloodline of the group. The early Israelites practiced endogamous marriage (Gen 24:3–4).

The biblical stories of finding a suitable wife contain details that offer a glimpse into some of ancient Israel's other social customs. This drama takes place at the well. As is the case in many patriarchal societies, procuring water for household use and for the care of animals was assigned to the women and/or children of the family. It was also customary for young women to go to the well to get water for the evening meal and for the night use. While the city gate was the major place where men gathered to conduct the business of the city, the common well was the place where the women congregated to converse and to exchange news as they drew water. It was at the common well just outside the city of Nahor that the first story about obtaining a wife unfolds.

In ancient patriarchal societies contact between women and men was rigorously controlled, because the reproductive potential of the family was held in the sexuality of the women. Men did not normally speak to women in public, not even to their wives. However, an exception was made at the well, because the need for water supersedes all other cultural considerations. That such stringent customs were set aside for the sake of obtaining water is noteworthy.

When Abraham's servant arrived at the well, a young woman appeared with her jug and the well-established ritual of hospitality took place. He asked for only a little water. It would be presumptuous to ask for more. On the other hand, the young woman, Rebekah, outdid herself in generosity, allowing this stranger to drink his fill of water. It would have been impolite to do otherwise. She then immediately attended to the needs of his animals, even without being asked to do so, for that too would have been expected. One camel normally needs about twenty gallons of water. The servant had ten camels, so this young woman was taking on a significant task in watering all the camels. Unbeknown to the servant, she was a relative of Abraham and, therefore, suitable for an endogamous marriage. The servant noted Rebekah's generosity in spirit, her enthusiasm in service, and her familiarity with the needs of animals. These were all admirable traits for a fitting wife in this culture.

A similar account is found in the Jacob cycle of stories (Gen 29:1–14). This time it was Jacob himself who, after a long journey, came upon a well that was frequently used by nomadic herders. The fact that these herders were from Haran, the home of Jacob's uncle Laban, indicates that the city was close by and that Jacob's journey was almost at its end. Droves of sheep were gathering around the well, but they were not yet being given water. Since the well was considered the common property of several herders, they waited for all of the flocks to arrive. This practice of waiting was probably meant to ensure that no one would take unfair advantage of the precious water. Laban's daughter Rachel, not one of his servants, brought his flock to the well. She came unattended, just as Rebekah had done before her, an acceptable custom for young women in charge of the flocks, especially when there are no sons in the family, as appears to have been case here. When Rachel arrived, Jacob himself rolled back the stone and watered the flock that Rachel had been tending.

In both courtship accounts the fundamental need for water superseded even the rigorously supervised customs regarding social exchange between women and men. Furthermore, human and animal interconnectedness and dependence on life-giving water created the circumstances for finding a suitable wife and ensuring the future of this people.

Living Water

Employing the hermeneutic of suspicion, we see that these passages do indeed underscore the intrinsic value of water. Not only were people dependent upon it for their survival, but its availability determined the route taken by the migrating ancestors of

Israel. One might even say that water set the course for the history of this people. Therefore, these passages have been retrieved without prejudice to their literary integrity. However, reading them from the perspective of the world in front of the text and through the community of Earth lens provides us with a different understanding, one that appreciates the essence of wholeness or fundamental catholicity.

The various sources of water that flow through the biblical story call to mind Earth's tender care for all of its living creatures. Plants, animals, and human beings thrive in their original environments, and with the help of other components of Earth, they learned to adjust to new environments. The challenges posed by new environments were great, sometimes overpowering. However, as the people traveled, they found that Earth supported them and provided them with the essentials of life. They viewed this as a sign of God's continual care for them despite these difficulties. To them, it may have seemed that God was intervening, acting directly in their lives. A modern reader will understand that God actually worked indirectly through the design and forces of the natural world.

While this section of the Bible is a story about one particular people, it is also the story about all people and about Earth itself. The story challenges us to examine our own attitudes toward water. We are so accustomed to using the components of Earth for our own purposes that we may fail to value them. In our consumption-driven society we often view these components as commodities, resources needed exclusively for our human projects, rather than as extraordinary expressions of Earth, interconnected and interdependent with other aspects of Earth, all of which possess value in themselves. We frequently use more water than we need, and we dispose of water that we do not use, seldom reflecting on the fact that millions of people suffer from the lack of water. Worse than this, we have polluted our water sources, our rivers and springs and wells, and in doing so we place in jeopardy the lives of all creatures dependent on these waters. Thus, our misuse of water is both an ecojustice and a social justice issue.

Earth itself has devised a mysterious and delicate balance whereby it continually renews itself. However, if we exploit the workings of nature without respecting the character and limits of these forces, we could throw the entire environmental balance into jeopardy. Nature can adjust to this mutation, but it might not produce an environment within which we and the life forms upon which we depend can adjust. All of Earth is governed by laws we did not devise, laws we cannot revise, laws to which we too are subject. Earth does not belong to us; we belong to Earth. We come from it; we are sustained by it; and in the end, we return to it.

We have only recently begun to realize the responsibility that is ours as decision-making Earth creatures. Both scientists and poets tell us that as part of Earth we are natural creation reflecting on itself. What an awesome way of characterizing human creatures. This idea calls to mind the amazement of the psalmist who cried out:

> What are human beings that you are mindful
> of them,
> mortals that you care for them? (Ps 8:4)

Still, as noble as our human nature might be, we can never forget that we are of Earth:

> You are dust, and to dust you shall return. (Gen 3:19)

We humans are a marvelous combination of dust and reflection, of what is material and what is nonmaterial. One of our unique traits is our ability to decide how we will live with and by means of the components of Earth that are so necessary for our surviving and our thriving. We can move beyond preoccupation with our own desires and projects and appreciate the broader picture, the ecosystem of which we are a part. We can develop attitudes of respect and concern for all the components of Earth. The stories of the Bible that we have been considering have something to teach us in this regard.

Though the Bible does not supply explicit answers to our questions, it does provide values that can inspire us, and it sets a direction for us to follow. The stories in this chapter call attention to the intrinsic value of water. They show that water's value is not determined simply by its usefulness to human beings. Rather, it is a fundamental component of the very structure of Earth; it is one of the treasures that have been provided for us. Furthermore, the importance of water for life points to the interconnectedness and interdependence of Earth components. It reminds us of nature's intrinsic catholicity or wholeness. Finally, our attitude toward our use of water has social implications. We can lay exclusive claims to it and risk the kind of social unrest that results from depriving people of what is essential for life, or we can devise ways of providing access to water for all. The biblical readings call us to an appreciation for and responsible guardianship of life-giving water.

Water, this very simple yet essential component of Earth, this vital component of our very physical being, might well be the fundamental property of life itself, for we have come to realize that the search for life elsewhere in the universe is actually the search for water.

"A land flowing with milk and honey"

—Joshua 5:6

Chapter Two

The land, the source of Israel's security and abundant harvests, plays a prominent role in the Historical Books (Joshua, Judges, 1 and 2 Samuel, 1 and 2 Kings). The first two books of this section tell the story of ancient Israel gaining possession of the land of Canaan. The other four books recount how the people lived in that land, eventually lost control of it, and were exiled from it to Babylon. This land is described as extraordinarily fertile: "flowing with milk and honey" (Exod 3:8, 17; 13:5; 33:3; Lev 20:24; Num 13:27; 14:8; 16:13, 14; Deut 6:3; 8:8; 11:9; 26:9, 15; 27:3; 31:10; 32:13; Josh 5:6). Throughout the Pentateuch we read that this land was promised by God to the ancestors, for example, "To your offspring I will give this land" (Gen 12:7). The people believed that this promise gave them the right to the land, even though other nations were living on it.

Despite Israel's claim to this land, they still held that it really belonged to God and was only theirs as an inheritance that had been freely given by God and could just as easily be taken back. In other words, Israel's occupancy of the land was conditional. As long as the people upheld the responsibilities that they willingly accepted when entering into covenant with God, they would be able to enjoy security within the land and benefit from its abundance. On the other hand, they maintained that infidelity on their part would result in their loss of these blessings. In this section of the Bible the land is considered a gift. An important aspect of this gift of land is its fruitfulness. The people's total dependence on this gift of land and their attitude toward it constitute the framework of this chapter in Israel's story.

Literary Context

The stories in the Book of Joshua give the impression that the ancestors of the Israelites took total control of the land of Canaan by means of three swift military attacks: the capture of Jericho and Ai in the central hill country of Canaan (Josh 6—7); a successful campaign against the kings in the southern part of the land (Josh 10); and the defeat of the kings in the north (Josh 11). However, the historical reliability of the report of their apparent success found in the Book of Joshua is thrown into question in the Book of Judges. There we read that these invaders repeatedly faced the opposition of the people who already lived in the land (Judg 2:11–23). This literary discrepancy has led to the development of various theories regarding the manner of Israel's occupation of the land of Canaan.

The traditional understanding presumes occupation that is primarily military. This view is based for the most part on a literal reading of the biblical stories found in the Book of Joshua and the archaeological evidence of ancient destruction. These stories recount how a group of people who escaped oppression in Egypt invaded and conquered the land of Canaan. Recent scholarship questions their historical reliability, primarily because a good deal of the archaeological dating does not correspond to details in the biblical stories. Current literary interpretation also challenges this position, insisting that the biblical narratives are really a form of theological reflection on events rather than precise historical reporting of them. They are considered by some as military stories that were very common in the Ancient Near East and were meant to enhance the dignity and power of the protective god and thus encourage trust and faithful commitment of the people.

A second scholarly position, which was put forward during the twentieth century, claims that occupation of Canaan resulted from gradual, peaceful infiltration into the land by various migrating tribes. This position argues that occupation resulted from one of the many population movements that occurred at the time in the Ancient Near East. While some conflict with the inhabitants of the land most probably occurred, it is believed that various political arrangements were formed that enabled those entering Canaan to settle in land that was most accessible to them, though probably least desirable from the point of view of the Canaanite inhabitants. Many biblical accounts reflect such a scenario.

A third theory regarding occupation holds that, while a small group of nomadic people entering the land might have instigated unrest, the Canaanite people themselves, who lived in the land under Egyptian domination, participated in a social revolution that resulted in a radical realignment of their political loyalties. A revolution of this type is recorded in ancient Egyptian documents. Today many commentators believe that aspects of each of these three theories describe the manner of Israel's occupation of the land of Canaan.

Once Israel achieved a foothold in Canaan, it was important for the people to retain control of the land. It soon became clear that relying solely on their own resources individual tribes would not be able to survive the threat posed by the Canaanites. Some form of cooperation among the tribes was necessary, along with a strong central figure who could assure this cooperation. Thus the people demanded: "Appoint for us, then, a king to govern us, like other nations" (1 Sam 8:5). The first king was Saul (1 Sam 11:15), a valiant military leader. He was followed by David (2 Sam 1:4; 5:3), a warrior who grew to be a shrewd administrator and who was able to consolidate the tribes in the south and then to gain the loyalties of those in the north. David's successor was his son Solomon. At Solomon's death, his son Rehoboam refused to lift the extraordinary burden of taxation imposed on the northern tribes by Solomon, and the people there revolted, seceded from the kingdom, and established their own government (1 Kgs 12:16). There were now two separate monarchies. The one in the south was known as the kingdom of Judah, taking its name from the largest southern tribe; the one in the north retained the name kingdom of Israel.

The northern kingdom of Israel lasted for about two hundred years (922–722 BCE), until the Assyrian army conquered it and deported many of its people (2 Kgs 17:6). The southern kingdom of Judah faced frequent threats of invasion and/or conquest.

However, it retained control over its land and people beyond the breakup of the northern tribes for about 140 years, until the more powerful armies of Babylon overran it, took possession of it, and carried many of its leading citizens into exile in Babylon (596–586 BCE; 2 Kgs 24:14). Like the people in the north, those in the south had now lost the land that God had promised to their ancestors. Furthermore, with the loss of their land they also lost an essential aspect of their very identity.

Mother Earth

All people need land upon which to live and from which to draw sustenance. Those who are truly landless, like exiles or refugees, lack the resources necessary for survival. They also lack social stability and suffer the loss of identity, since they are not identified with the land in which they live. They are vulnerable and totally dependent on others. While actual ownership of land is not always necessary, access to land is. For example, nomadic people do not possess the land that supports them. However, they do have access to some portion of the land and to the riches found there. It is only in this way that they are able to survive.

Land, or Earth, possesses mysterious powers. As from a womb, it brings forth plant life in cornucopian variety. This fact of nature is captured in the first creation account:

> The earth brought forth vegetation: plants yielding seed
> of every kind, and trees of every kind bearing fruit with
> the seed in it. And God saw that it was good. (Gen 1:12)

Furthermore, Earth continues to nourish from its very substance the diverse forms of life that it brings forth. It is no wonder that land is often referred to as Mother Earth. The mysterious life properties of Earth and the interconnectedness of forms of life that come from Earth have long been recognized by poets and scientists alike.

Turning to the Bible, we see that the attitude of ancient Israel toward land varied, depending upon the political and/or social circumstances within which the people found themselves. When the people were landless nomads, the land was viewed as a gift from God; once settled in the land, they considered it an inheritance for which they were responsible and accountable to God. At times the fruitfulness of the land was seen as a blessing; at other times the same fruitfulness became a temptation. Finally, because of their understanding of the covenant that God had made with them, the people interpreted loss of land as punishment for their disregard of that covenant commitment.

Gift

From the very beginning of Israel's story, land was considered a gift promised by God. This promise was made first to Abram:

> "To your offspring I will give this land." (Gen 12:7)

then to his son Isaac:

> "For to you and to your descendants I will give all these lands." (Gen 26:3)

and to Isaac's son Jacob:

> "The land on which you lie I will give to you and to your offspring." (Gen 28:13)

Finally, this promise of land was renewed when God made a covenant at Sinai with the entire people who were brought out of Egyptian bondage:

> God also spoke to Moses and said to him: "I am the LORD: I appeared to Abraham, Isaac, and Jacob as God Almighty, but by my name 'The LORD' I did not make myself known to them. I also established my covenant with them, to give them the land of Canaan, the land in which they resided as aliens. (Exod 6:2–4)

Though the land was considered a gift from God, conditions were set for the people's continued enjoyment of this gift. God had initiated a covenant or mutual agreement of commitment with the people (see Exod 19:3–6). As part of this agreement, the people were expected to live in faithfulness to its stipulations. Having entered into this solemn pact with God, they were now considered God's special people, and they were to act accordingly. God's commitment to the people included a promise of land:

> Keep, then, this entire commandment that I am commanding you today, so that you may have strength to go in and occupy the land that you are crossing over to occupy, and so that you may live long in the land that the LORD swore to your ancestors to give them and to their descendants, a land flowing with milk and honey. (Deut 11:8–9)

The land that was first promised to the ancestors, then promised anew to the people who had come out of Egyptian bondage, was given to those who had crossed the Jordan River into Canaan:

> Thus the LORD gave to Israel all the land that he swore to their ancestors that he would give them; and having taken possession of it, they settled there. (Josh 21:43)

The idea of the land as a gift from God, given out of divine generosity, corresponds to the contemporary idea of creation evolving out of the graciousness of its divine source. A gift is never earned; it is freely given as an expression of love. All that it requires is that the one receiving the gift accept it with gratitude, acknowledge and value it for what it really is, and show respect for it and for the giver by using it as it is intended to be used. Viewing the land as gift meant that the people not assume that they enjoyed exclusive proprietorship with unrestrained exercise of authority over the use of the land. Furthermore, this land was not given to individuals but to a people, who together were both responsible for its flourishing and accountable for it to God. These characteristics are consistent with the ecojustice principles of intrinsic value and mutual custodianship.

Inheritance

Regardless of how one understands the manner in which ancient Israel occupied the land of Canaan, it is clear that the people never really claimed the land as theirs by right. Rather, they believed that it belonged to God. They were told to "cross over into the LORD's land" (Josh 22:19). Their insistence that the land belonged to God might explain why in this section of the Bible the land is seldom referred to as the land of Israel. Nonetheless, the people did enjoy a special relationship with the land, and the word most frequently used to describe this relationship is *inheritance:*

> So Joshua took the whole land, according to all that the LORD had spoken to Moses; and Joshua gave it for an inheritance to Israel according to their tribal allotments. (Josh 11:23)

This word, *inheritance,* is used in various ways in different biblical passages. Consequently, its exact meaning is not always clear. Some commentators claim that inheritance refers to the actual property that is handed down from generation to generation. This understanding is challenged because, in the Book of Joshua, where the word is most frequently found,[1] the inheritance is assigned by God to an entire tribe as an allotment or portion of land on which that tribe would live, not merely as property willed to an heir at the death of a close relative, as inheritance is usually understood today. Perhaps the best way to understand how ancient Israel viewed inheritance is as an entitlement or right to property, rather than as the actual property itself. The portion of property assigned to each tribe is then considered its allotment. This would mean that God's promise of land to the ancestors gave their descendants a right to the land in which they would eventually settle.

The Book of Joshua states the general assignment of land first. The Lord told Joshua:

> "Now therefore divide this land for an inheritance to the nine tribes and the half-tribe of Manasseh."
> With the other half-tribe of Manasseh the Reubenites and the Gadites received their inheritance, which Moses

---

[1] Appearances of this word are too numerous to cite. It is found almost fifty times in the accounts of the allotment of land to the various tribes alone (Josh 13—19).

gave them, beyond the Jordan eastward, as Moses the servant of the LORD gave them. (Josh 13:7–8)

This declaration is followed by descriptions of specific allotments of land to each individual tribe (Josh 13—19). The allotment of land reflects a practice of feudal land grants that was popular in the Ancient Near East. In it, a feudal lord granted land to a tenant. This grant required specific services from the tenant in return. Though land grants were given to the tenants, the land always belonged to the feudal lord. Ancient Israel transferred this social practice to a theological plane, thus giving religious meaning to the practice and bestowing religious significance to the land. These land grants or allotments were always conditional, dependent on the people's conformity to the obligations to which they agreed when they entered into covenant with God:

> "If you transgress the covenant of the LORD your God, which he enjoined on you . . . you shall perish quickly from the good land that he has given to you." (Josh 23:16)

The understanding of inheritance and land grants highlights some important theological concepts. First, God is the sole owner of the land. Second, human beings are tenant settlers with both responsibility for the land and accountability to God. Third, the gift of land is conditional; it will be enjoyed only by the people if they are faithful to their covenant commitment. Various ecojustice concepts enhance our appreciation of land as inheritance. Land tenure was granted because of the need of the human settlers. They were totally dependent on the land; the land was not dependent on them. In other words, there was no doubt about its intrinsic value. Furthermore, land tenure was granted to the entire tribe, both those alive at the time and future descendants. This corresponds to the ecojustice principle of mutual custodianship.

Possession

Although the land is generally referred to as gift or inheritance, there are passages where it is called a possession that was seized by means of force (Josh 12:6–7). While the Hebrew word for seize comes from the verb that is sometimes translated inherit, it means to inherit for oneself by disinheriting another. This idea is very disturbing for some contemporary readers, not primarily because of the violence implied, but because the land was forcibly taken from those already inhabiting it. These readers find it very difficult to defend what they see as an invasion and land theft. Even more troublesome are the explicit statements that it was God who gave the land of Canaan to the people to lay siege to and to possess (Deut 19:24; 21:1; 25:19; Josh 1:11). Some passages even say that God aggressively cleared away the nations before them (Deut 7:1; 11:23; 31:3).

Various attempts to soften the severity of these passages have been advanced. Some claim that most of them are found in the Book of Deuteronomy, an exilic or postexilic book that interpreted earlier traditions through the lens of retribution theology. Thus, the historicity of the passages is doubtful. This argument might minimize the historical possibility of military activity, but it raises several serious theological questions. First, it thrusts to center stage the scandal of particularity—Israel's privileged position among all other people. It is one thing to say that Israel was chosen over all other nations to enter into covenant with God; it is quite another to claim that God takes an actual stand in favor of Israel and against other people. The reason given for this preference is found in the Bible itself:

> It is not because of your righteousness or the uprightness of your heart that you are going in to occupy their land; but because of the wickedness of these nations the LORD your God is dispossessing them before you, in order to fulfill the promise that the LORD made on oath to your ancestors, to Abraham, to Isaac, and to Jacob. (Deut 9:5)

Still, this reason lacks persuasiveness, for the people led by God were just as guilty of sin as were the Canaanites, perhaps even more so, for these invaders were bound to God by the intimate ties of covenant. So why did God choose one unfaithful people over another? One might say that the Bible is, after all, the story of Israel as told by Israel itself. One would expect Israel to be portrayed as chosen. While this is true, it does not address the thorny question: Does God really have favorites?

According to this text God allowed, even directed, the people to take the land of the Canaanites because of the earlier promise God made to Abraham, Isaac, and Jacob. One might still ask: Is the fulfillment of a promise made to one people reason enough to victimize another? A positive answer casts God into the guise of a capricious deity.

Second, these passages present God as extraordinarily violent:

> Know then today that the LORD your God is the one who crosses over before you as a devouring fire; he will defeat them and subdue them before you, so that you may dispossess and destroy them quickly, as the LORD has promised you. (Deut 9:3)

This violence is not simply forceful, as we understand the energies of nature to be. Rather, it is a violence that is explicitly directed against a people. Furthermore, the brutal seizing of land not only pits God against the Canaanites, but against Earth as well. War maims and destroys Earth and all living creatures of Earth. The land is scarred by the ravages of such violence, and these passages describe God as the perpetrator. Moreover, the people of God are directed to participate in violence. By attributing this violence to God, it is awarded religious sanction.

Perceiving the land as a possession seized from those already living on it violates all of the ecojustice principles. In this scenario:

1. The land is regarded as a commodity to be taken from another if need be. Any value it may possess in itself is disregarded. The needs or desires of the invaders are uppermost.

2. There is no thought of the interconnectedness of the members of the community of Earth or of the interdependence that naturally flows from it. The invader is supreme.

3. Earth has no voice; there is no reason to consider its needs or well-being.

4. The plans and strategies of the invaders supersede any overall goals of a broader cosmic design.

5. There is no thought of responsibility for the delicate ecological balance on Earth and the creatures that rely on the bounty of Earth. Therefore, there is no regard for custodianship or stewardship.

6. Though Earth and Earth creatures suffer from the ravages of war, they are unable to resist them. Consequently, Earth's ability to regenerate living forms is diminished with each military encounter.

Some have tried to salvage the idea of land as a possession seized by God or by the people of God following God's directive by insisting that the historical details are highly exaggerated. However, the stories are what have been handed down as scripture, and they appear to justify violence. Other commentators focus on God's obvious unbounded care for the ancestors of the Israelites. However, even that positive concept is wedded to the idea that the price of that care was paid by another people. The passages persist in being troublesome. Perhaps all one can say is that the tradition of land as a possession is historically conditioned by the cultural practices and understandings of that time rather than revelatory for all times. Commentators might not know what to do with this tradition, but no one doubts that its obvious meaning should not be replicated.

The Good Land

The early promises repeatedly describe Canaan as "a land flowing with milk and honey" (Exod 3:8, 17; 13:5; 33:3; Lev 20:24; Num 13:27; 14:8; 16:13, 14; Deut 6:3; 11:9; 26:9, 15; 27:3; 31:20). A passage in Deuteronomy is quite explicit in this description:

> For the LORD your God is bringing you into a good land, a land with flowing streams, with springs and underground waters welling up in valleys and hills, a land of wheat and barley, of vines and fig trees and pomegranates, a land of olive trees and honey, a land where you may eat bread

without scarcity, where you will lack nothing, a land whose stones are iron and from whose hills you may mine copper. You shall eat your fill and bless the LORD your God for the good land that he has given you. (Deut 8:7–10)

The expression "a land flowing with milk and honey" points to the fertility of the land, where agriculture, animal husbandry, and viticulture all thrive. The image grew out of the people's experience of the products that were derived from the fruitfulness of the land. Milk is probably a reference to the milk of sheep and goats, which was usually curdled in order to produce curds and cheese; honey may refer to its use in preserving grape juice, which was kept as a thick, sugary syrup. This land was, and continues to be, truly a land of promise, not only because it was pledged to the people by God, but also because of the possibilities of rich yield hidden deep within it. Though this land contained mineral wealth as well, the people would thrive primarily through animal husbandry (milk) and agriculture (honey).

The climate of Canaan was subtropical and dependent on annual rainfall. There were only two seasons, the dry summer and the rainy season. Though most of the rain fell between November and February, there was no period of the year when the land did not yield some crop. In 1908 a small limestone plaque was discovered at the site of Gezer, an ancient Canaanite city about twenty miles west of Jerusalem. This plaque, known as the Gezer Calendar, contains a poem describing Israel's agricultural operations, starting with today's September and October:

> His first months are (olive) harvest,
> His two months are planting (grain),
> His two months are late planting;
> His month is hoeing of flax,
> His month is harvest of barley,
> His month is harvest and feasting;
> His two months are vine-tending,
> His month is summer fruit.[2]

---

[2] Philip J. King and Lawrence E. Stager, *Life in Biblical Israel* (Louisville, KY: Westminster John Knox, 2001), 87–88.

Scholars are not sure of the original purpose of this ancient plaque. It may have been designed as some kind of formula used for collecting taxes from farmers, or it could have been a school tablet meant to aid in memorization. Whatever the case might have been, the Gezer Calendar provides a glimpse into the diversity of agricultural activity and the products brought forth from the land, products that included grains, fruits, and vegetables. The listing of two major harvest periods is evidence of the fertility of the land.

The land also supported various forms of animal husbandry. The cultivated plants that had been coaxed out of the land became the food for domesticated animals. While more than a hundred animals are named in the Bible, only a few of them were domesticated by the people. Chief among them were the sheep and the goats:

> There was a man in Maon, whose property was in Carmel. The man was very rich; he had three thousand sheep and a thousand goats. (1 Sam 25:2)

Sheep were raised primarily for their wool, which not only clothed the people but also served as a valuable commodity in commerce. Wool production led to other occupations, like dyeing and weaving. Sheep also produced meat and hides. Because of the value of sheep, the poor were more likely to slaughter and consume goats than sheep. Goats produced meat, clothing, and twice the amount of milk produced by sheep. Goat hair and hides were used for clothing and tents. Goats' milk produced products like curds and cheese. Goat skins were used to make containers for water and oil. Finally, both sheep and goats were acceptable as sacrificial animals in Israel's worship.

Other animals were important less for the products they yielded than for the work they could do. This was true of horses, which were used primarily with chariots in battle and in royal or cultic processions:

> Solomon's import of horses was from Egypt and Kue, and the king's traders received them from Kue at a price. A chariot could be imported from Egypt for six hundred shekels of silver, and a horse for one hundred fifty;

so through the king's traders they were exported to all
the kings of the Hittites and the kings of Aram. (1 Kgs
10:28–29)

Donkeys and mules were employed as work animals:

Jesse took a donkey loaded with bread, a skin of wine,
and a kid, and sent them by his son David to Saul. (1 Sam
16:20)

as means of transportation:

Then he said to his sons, "Saddle a donkey for me." So
they saddled a donkey for him, and he mounted it. (1 Kgs
13:13)

and in various official functions:

> Rejoice greatly, O daughter Zion!
>   Shout aloud, O daughter Jerusalem!
> Lo, your king comes to you; triumphant and
>   victorious is he,
>   humble and riding on a donkey, on a colt,
>   the foal of a donkey. (Zech 9:9)

Camels were also used as beasts of burden:

So Hazael went to meet him, taking a present with him, all
kinds of goods of Damascus, forty camel loads. (2 Kgs 8:9)

All of this bounty and diversity was possible because of the
fertility of the land. These passages demonstrate the interconnectedness existing between and among all of the components of
Earth, as well as their dependence on one another. Earth brings
forth this abundance and then provides for it from its own nutri-
tious substance. This fruitfulness will continue as long as each
member of the community of Earth makes its unique and necessary contribution and makes room for the unique and necessary
contributions of other members.

Land Sabbath

Despite the fertility of the land, farming was a challenge for ancient Israel. Farmers had to contend with the unpredictability of winds and rains as well as the diversity in soil composition. Hence, diversified farming became very popular. It allowed farmers to stagger sowing and harvesting, thus spreading out their work over the entire agricultural season, as the Gezer Calendar indicates. This slowed the depletion of nutrients as well as the damage done by crop disease. The climate also made what has come to be known as dryland farming almost a necessity. This form of farming includes the fallow system of farming, a practice dating from ancient times. The term *fallow* refers to land that is plowed but left unseeded during a growing season. This practice enables the land to refurbish its moisture content, rebalance soil nutrients within it, reestablish natural soil forms of plant and animal life, break cycles of crop pest infestation and disease, and provide a haven for wildlife. The fallow land system enables land to regenerate itself.

While allowing the land to lie fallow was a wise agrarian practice, it also brought great risks. When farming was almost a subsistence enterprise and produce was in great demand, fallow land practice could deprive the people and their animals of necessary food for a long period of time. It is no wonder that this practice took on religious meaning. While it is true that fallow land is rich in potential productivity, though inactive for a time, and that it rejuvenates itself while it is resting, it requires trust in the providence of God. The religious meaning of the fallow land practice is found in two places in the Bible, in Exodus and in Leviticus. These passages direct the way the people are to live in the land once they have entered it. The Exodus passage probably contains the earlier tradition:

> For six years you may sow your land and gather in its yield; but the seventh year you shall let it rest and lie fallow, so that the poor of your people may eat; and what they leave the wild animals may eat. You shall do the same with your vineyard, and with your olive orchard. (Exod 23:10–11)

While the fundamental purpose of the fallow land system was ecological, allowing Earth's natural forces to replenish themselves, the focus in this Exodus passage is humanitarian, underscoring the Israelites' responsibility to care for the needy in their midst. Elsewhere this same humanitarian reason is given for observance of sabbath day rest:

> But the seventh day is the sabbath of the LORD your God; you shall not do any work—you, or your son or your daughter, or your male or female slave, or your ox or your donkey, or any of your livestock, or the resident alien in your towns, so that your male and female slave may rest as well as you. Remember that you were a slave in the land of Egypt, and the LORD your God brought you out from there with a mighty hand and an outstretched arm; therefore the LORD your God commanded you to keep the sabbath day. (Deut 5:14–15)

Sabbath rest, whether it is rest of people or rest of the land, was observed in order to remind the Israelites of the sovereignty of God and their dependence on that sovereignty. It underscored their belief that though the land was occupied and worked by people, it really belonged to God; all the people rested in order to remember that their labor in tending that land did not assure them prosperity, but it was the graciousness of God that gave them this land "flowing with milk and honey."

A third focus on this system of farming is found in a passage from Leviticus. It offers a theological reason for the people to allow land to lie fallow:

> The LORD spoke to Moses on Mount Sinai saying: Speak to the People of Israel and say to them: When you enter the land that I am giving you the land shall observe a sabbath for the LORD. Six years you shall sow your field, and six years you shall prune your vineyard, and gather in their yield; but in the seventh year there shall be a sabbath of complete rest for the land, a sabbath for the LORD: you shall not sow your field or prune your vineyard. (Lev 25:1–4)

This passage commands complete rest for the land. While the earlier Exodus passage allows the poor to gather any aftergrowth that the fallow land might produce, this directive from Leviticus forbids that practice; any aftergrowth is to remain in the fallow land. Most important, the period in which the land is to lie fallow is identified as "a sabbath for the LORD."

This fallow land practice, therefore, can be viewed in at least three different ways. First, it had a fundamental ecological importance, allowing the land to rejuvenate itself. Second, humanitarian concerns for the less fortunate members of the community were added to this basic understanding, directing those responsible for the farming to allow the poor to gather some of the produce. Third, the practice acquired a profound theological interpretation, which reminded the people that the land really belongs to God, and God, not simply their farming efforts, would provide for them. It is clear from this that the land is meant to serve those who work it; it should also benefit those who are poor or needy; but most important, land serves God. In this way the land is seen as a living reality. The fallow land practice required trust in God. By means of it, the economic security that was usually rooted in the growing potential of fertile land was transformed into trust in God's providential care. This turn to the providence of God also indicated the true ownership of the land. This land was God's by right; the human landowner was considered only a tenant farmer. Land sabbath was meant to remind the people of this profound religious truth.

The religious meaning of the fallow land system is grounded in the sabbath tradition. This tradition includes the practice of observing the Jubilee year and its prescription of land sabbath:

> That fiftieth year shall be a jubilee year for you: you shall not sow, or reap the aftergrowth, or harvest the unpruned vines. For it is a jubilee; it shall be holy to you: you shall eat only what the field itself produces. (Lev 25:11–12)

This sabbath tradition is rich and wide ranging. It includes observance of the sabbath day, the sabbath year, and the Jubilee year. Just as the seventh day of the week is a day of rest, so the seventh year is a year of rest, and the year after seven sets of seven years (the fiftieth year) is a year of rest and return. Sabbath theology informs all aspects of this tradition. Whether the development of the concept of sabbath rest originated with observance of the sabbath day and developed into marking the year and then the Jubilee year (fiftieth year) is not clear.[3] However, all these observances highlight many of the same ecological, humanitarian, and theological themes.

A purely anthropocentric evaluation of Earth exploits its riches until it can no longer produce, then casts it aside and looks for other resources. Respect for Earth means not only appreciation for its fruitfulness, but also sensitivity to its limits. The various expressions of the sabbath tradition underscore this respect, acknowledging the intrinsic value of Earth and all members of the community of Earth.

Land Management

The land that was first promised to the ancestors by God was ultimately regarded by the people as an inheritance that they had to manage. Since it was believed to be God's land and merely entrusted to the people on condition of their loyalty, the management of the land was considered a serious responsibility. While the land was under the jurisdiction of specific tribes, the borders of fields were left unharvested so that those who were landless for any reason at all could benefit from the fruitfulness of the land of another. The story of Ruth illustrates this practice. In the book that bears her name, the Moabite Ruth is directed by her mother-in-law, Naomi, to glean in the fields of a man named Boaz, a relative of her deceased father-in-law:

> She went and gleaned in the field behind the reapers. As it happened she came to the part of the field belonging to Boaz, who was of the family of Elimelech. (Ruth 2:3)

This practice of allowing the poor to glean in the field of another not only gives evidence of ancient Israel's care for those in their

---

[3] Richard H. Lowery, *Sabbath and Jubilee* (St. Louis: Chalice Press, 2000), 5.

midst who were less fortunate, but it also demonstrates the conviction that the land and all of its produce really belong to God and are meant for the benefit of the entire people.

A change of government structure modified many of the practices of land management. At the time of the monarchy, land management was presided over by the king. This does not mean that the monarchy took possession of the land. Individuals and tribes still exercised a certain degree of authority. However, it became the king's responsibility to make sure that their land rights were respected. This is made clear in a story that recounts King Ahab's attempt to purchase a plot of land containing a vineyard that was adjacent to his property. This land belonged to a man named Naboth (1 Kgs 21). The king wanted to convert the vineyard into a vegetable garden for himself and his household. Naboth refused to sell, stating: "The LORD forbid that I should give you my ancestral inheritance" (1 Kgs 21:3). Urged by his Phoenician wife, Jezebel, King Ahab falsely accused Naboth of serious crimes, had him executed, and then claimed the land for the monarchy. However, this evil did not go unnoticed or unpunished:

> Then the word of the LORD came to Elijah the Tishbite, saying, Go down to meet King Ahab of Israel, who rules in Samaria; he is now in the vineyard of Naboth, where he has gone to take possession. You shall say to him, "Thus says the LORD: Have you killed, and also taken possession?" You shall say to him, "Thus says the LORD: In the place where dogs licked up the blood of Naboth, dogs will also lick up your blood." (1 Kgs 21:17–19)

The terrible fate that awaited the king because of his violation of the land rights of a simple man underscores the seriousness of those rights. King Ahab's defiance was not merely a violation of Naboth's rights, but it was also an affront to the sovereignty of God, who was the real landowner.

Though the monarchy provided a degree of political security for the people, it was not an unmixed blessing. The kings gradually patterned the structures and trappings of their monarchy after the kingdoms of other Ancient Near Eastern rulers. The warning pronounced earlier by the prophet Samuel, when the people had grown tired of the limited and ineffectual leadership of the judges and demanded a king, soon came to pass:

> So Samuel reported all the words of the LORD to the people who were asking him for a king. He said, "These will be the ways of the king who will reign over you: he will take your sons and appoint them to his chariots and to be his horsemen, and to run before his chariots; and he will appoint for himself commanders of thousands and commanders of fifties, and some to plow his ground to reap his harvest, and to make his implements of war and the equipment of his chariots. He will take your daughters to be perfumers and cooks and bakers. He will take the best of your fields and vineyards and olive orchards and give them to his courtiers. He will take one-tenth of your grain and of your vineyards and give it to his officers and his courtiers. He will take your male and female slaves, and the best of your cattle and donkeys, and put them to his work. He will take one-tenth of your flocks, and you shall be his slaves. And in that day you will cry out because of your king, whom you have chosen for ourselves; but the LORD will not answer you in that day." (1 Sam 8:10–18)

The kingdom that was meant to function as a kind of household with God at its head gradually grew to resemble an empire with despotic rulers as its leaders. The land that belonged to God alone and was intended as an inheritance for the entire people was soon looked upon as the personal fiefdom of the royal leaders. Both the tribal leaders and the people who clamored for a king closed their eyes to their failure to uphold the covenant responsibilities to which they freely committed themselves. By doing this, they had placed in jeopardy themselves and the very land on which they lived and upon which their well-being depended.

Even before the land was ultimately lost to foreign nations, it suffered in various ways because of the sinfulness of the people. If fertility and abundance were seen as blessings from God, drought and barrenness were considered punishments. However, in drought and barrenness the land itself was stricken. In one instance David acts against the will of God and is told to choose his punishment:

> The word of the LORD came to the prophet Gad, David's
> seer, saying, "Go and say to David: Thus says the LORD:
> Three things I offer you; choose one of them, and I will do
> it to you." So Gad came to David and told him; he asked
> him, "Shall three years of famine come to you on your
> land? Or will you flee three months before your foes while
> they pursue you? Or shall there be three days' pestilence
> in your land?" (2 Sam 24:12–13)

Many commentators praise David for choosing the shortest suffering, the three days' pestilence. However, in doing so, they over-
look the fact that the land is victimized in that punishment. Had
David chosen the second option, only he would have suffered,
not the land and the rest of his people, who were dependent on
the land for their lives.

On the occasion of the dedication of the Temple, Solomon
asks that the prayers lifted to God from the Temple might remedy natural disasters that result from human sin:

> When heaven is shut up and there is no rain because they
> have sinned against you . . . then hear in heaven and forgive
> the sin of your servants . . . and grant rain on your land,
> which you have given to your people as an inheritance. If
> there is famine in the land, if there is plague, blight, mildew,
> locust or caterpillar . . . then hear in heaven your dwelling
> place, forgive . . . so that they may fear you all the days
> that they live in the land that you gave to our ancestors.
> (1 Kgs 8:35–40)

It is clear that even at the time of the monarchy, the people
acknowledged that the land and its fruits belonged to God and
were Israel's only as an inheritance.

These last passages show that Israel believed that God employed components of nature to reward them for their faithfulness and punish them for infidelity.[4] This suggests that the
balance in nature is governed by moral law rather than by scientific laws. While this thinking might have provided the ancient

---

[4] Even today many people hold that natural disaster is a punishment
from God.

Israelites with an explanation for natural disaster and an impetus to remain faithful to their covenant responsibilities, it portrays God in a very negative light, setting aside any thought of the intrinsic value of the natural world as was stated at the time of creation: "And God saw that it was good" (Gen 1:10, 12, 18, 21, 25); "It was very good" (Gen 1:31). This negative image of God is solidly embedded in the religious thinking of both ancient Israel and early Christianity alike. All the modern reader can do is to acknowledge that such a portrayal is culturally conditioned by an unscientific understanding of the cosmos. Here again we see what was stated in the Introduction to this study: "People's understanding of the origin, structure, makeup, and working of the universe has influenced how they perceive human nature, its place and role within that universe, and divinity and its power and control over that universe." New scientific insights into the universe should lay to rest this ancient concept of a God who uses elements of the natural world to punish.

Today, we know that human actions can indeed alter the balance of the forces of nature. However, we now realize that this is because we are an integral part of that balance, interconnected with all other members of the community of Earth. Consequently, through our thoughtless, selfish, greedy actions we are responsible for much of the pollution in the air and the water; we have contributed to the global warming that has caused much of the dramatic climate change resulting in drought, tornadoes, and torrential flooding. What might be devastating for human beings is really nature working according to its fundamental laws, making adjustments to human behavior. This might further trouble some who ask: Why doesn't God step in and prevent this suffering? Evolutionary thinking today argues that God works through the forces and laws of nature, not against them. One might say, then, by allowing nature to function in this way, God is really respecting its intrinsic value.

Loss of Land

During the reign of Rehoboam, the son of Solomon, the northern tribes severed their allegiance to that southern king. They were now an independent kingdom. However, continued internal strife and constant threats from Assyria to the north finally wore down their resistance. The kingdom was defeated by Assyria and was transformed from being an independent state to being a vassal of its conqueror:

> King Shalmaneser Assyria came up against him; Hoshea became his vassal, and paid him tribute. (2 Kgs 17:3)

The riches of the land that belonged to God were now laid at the feet of a foreign king who paid homage to a foreign god. Eventually that Assyrian king invaded the kingdom of Israel and carried many of the people away to Assyria. This defeat was interpreted as just punishment for the sins of the people in the northern kingdom:

> This occurred because the people of Israel had sinned against the LORD their God. (2 Kgs 17:7)

The southern kingdom of Judah was spared at this time. However, as was the case with the northern kingdom, the land in the south suffered, as did the innocent living creatures dependent on it:

> How long will the land mourn,
>   and the grass of every field wither?
> For the wickedness of those who live in it
>   the animals and the birds are swept away.
>   (Jer 12:4)

Eventually, the southern kingdom found itself caught in a power struggle between Egypt to the southwest and Babylon to the northeast. This struggle between foreign kings was reflected in the tension within the politics of the government in Jerusalem. Some of the people there supported the Babylonian cause, while others favored Egypt. When Babylonian forces finally defeated Egypt, Jerusalem paid dearly for having favored that defeated nation. Over the course of ten years (597–587 BCE), the kingdom of Judah suffered three different deportations; finally, the city of Jerusalem was destroyed. Though the Babylonians were the ones who devastated the land and the city, it was believed that it was Israel's violation of the land that made such devastation possible. Speaking through the prophet Jeremiah, God declared:

> "I brought you into a plentiful land
>   to eat its fruits and its good things.
> But when you entered you defiled my land,
>   and made my heritage an abomination."
>   (Jer 2:7)

Since the Hebrew word for defile generally points to a ritual situation, this defilement or pollution refers to false worship rather than to environmental contamination. Israel has turned to the worship of other gods, thus turning its back on the God who brought them into the land in the first place.

The story about land in the Historical Books begins with the land being given as gift and ends with that gift being violated and thrown away. It is a story of divine graciousness and generosity and human ingratitude and sin. Although the people eventually return to the land, their attitude toward it is never quite the same again. From this point on, land takes on another meaning. Added to the well-established importance of the actual land is a symbolic meaning of land as fulfillment in the future.

Commentators today acknowledge that the loss of the land resulted from conquest by the stronger military forces of the Babylonians rather than from direct punishment by God, as the Israelites probably thought. This position might explain actual historical events, but contemporary believers must still address the revelatory value of biblical texts that see misfortune as divine retribution. It will be through critical historical examination of such texts that their culturally determined images and manner of expression will be separated from their fundamental religious message. Only then can the intrinsic value of the community of Earth be respected and the image of a caring and provident God be retrieved.

Responsibility for Land

With the exception of a few traditional tribes, most people in today's world have a very different understanding of individual land rights than that found in the biblical tradition. Plots of land are viewed as legal possessions, and individuals readily buy and sell them. At issue here is not the sense of possession of the land, but the attitudes we have toward land itself. People often think: The land is mine and I can do with it whatever I want. Or, The land only has value if it is profitable, or if it serves my needs and interests. It is attitudes like these that have resulted in the exploitation and pollution of Earth. Such attitudes might be remedied by most of the attitudes toward land found in the Bible. The positive views can be easily retrieved and refocused. However, those that are negative pose serious problems.

First and foremost is the Bible's insistence that the land is really God's and only freely given to human beings as a gift, as an inheritance to be cared for. Thus it does not belong to human beings to do with as they please. Individuals might exercise land rights, but they also have serious responsibilities when it comes to ecological systems and limits. The observance of various sabbatical practices is evidence of ancient Israel's realization of this fact. Furthermore, because of the fundamental connectedness or oneness of land, the way one plot is used or misused has repercussions in adjoining or even distant lands. Finally, the true value of the land is not dependent on its ability to provide sustenance and wealth for human beings. Rather, it is valuable in itself as having been brought forth by God. Understanding land in this way challenges many contemporary attitudes. However, many policies of land protection and sustainability are being enacted throughout the world in an attempt to remedy destructive attitudes and behavior.

Second, Earth is a community of interconnected and interdependent creatures. Too often we think that living creatures, both plants and animals, depend for their survival on the efforts that human beings invest in various forms of agriculture and managing livestock. Actually, all life forms, including human beings, are dependent on Earth, not the other way around. The early Israelites had to learn the life-producing possibilities of the land on which they lived as well as the patterns of weather that affected them if they were to survive and thrive on that land. The Gezer Calendar demonstrates their ability to adjust to their place on Earth. Societies that are immediately dependent on the productivity of Earth are usually more aware of this interconnectedness and interdependence than are city dwellers. However, water, land, and air pollution as well as the effects of climate change have brought a realization of the oneness of the natural world to the forefront of the lives of all. We all have much to relearn in this area. Such reeducation calls us back to the ancient Greeks awareness of this oneness, to which they ascribed the word *catholic*.

Finally, the productivity of the land and of the living creatures of that land was intimately linked with the people's fidelity to their freely taken covenant obligations. When the people were unfaithful, the innocent land and those dependent on it suffered the consequences along with the guilty human beings. This is evident in experiences of drought, famine, the death of animals, and then of destruction and conquest of the land first by the Assyrians and then by the Babylonians. One might see this as an injustice. After all, it was the humans who dishonored the covenant, not the rest of creation. However, this shared affliction illustrates the interconnectedness or intrinsic wholeness of all creatures of Earth. When one aspect of Earth suffers, all of Earth suffers. Once again we have come to realize this because of ecological disasters. A reexamination of Lovelock's Gaia Hypothesis will probably benefit us all.

While biblical passages that speak of land as gift or inheritance can be retrieved and continue to provide religious meaning, those stories that describe the seizure of the land from people already living on it pose a problem for today. As already discussed, such stories are too historically conditioned by the cultural practices and understandings of that time to be considered revelatory for all times, and they cannot be rehabilitated. They must be set aside.

"Thus says the LORD"

—Amos 1:3

Chapter Three

As discussed in the previous chapter, the land upon which ancient Israel eventually settled was referred to as "a land flowing with milk and honey" (Josh 5:6). The people who migrated from Mesopotamia and eventually settled in this land formed themselves into a loosely organized social and political union that came to be known as the tribes of Jacob. This form of organization allowed the people a significant degree of tribal independence, while at the same time it was meant to guarantee them the assurance of mutual support whenever that support was deemed necessary. However, they soon realized that they would not be able to endure the domination of more powerful nations if they did not accept some form of centralized government that could unify their holdings and consolidate their energies. In the ancient world such political organization would be some form of monarchy. Accepting a monarchy presented a serious dilemma for the people, for their very identity was grounded in their past deliverance by God from the tyrannical grip of the royal Egyptian pharaoh. To accept a human king was seen by some as turning their back on the deity to whom they had promised undivided allegiance.

Those advocating a monarchy won the day. They brought their demand for a king to the prophet Samuel, who was their religious leader. Samuel was opposed to the idea and warned them sternly:

"[The king] will take the best of your fields and vineyards and olive orchards and give them to his courtiers. He will take one-tenth of your grain and of your vineyards and give it to his officials and courtiers. He will take your male and female slaves, and the best of your cattle and donkeys, and put them to his work. He will take one-tenth of your flocks, and you will be his slaves." (1 Sam 8:14–17)

What a dire picture of the monarchy is painted here. Many commentators believe that this passage is less a look into the future than a description of monarchy as it eventually developed during the time of Solomon. In either case it underscores the abuses of Earth and the products of Earth of which this form of government was guilty. This was a people who took great pride in the idea that God intended that they should enjoy the fruits of the land that God had allotted to them. The relinquishment of the fruits of that land became the price that they were forced to pay for a monarch. Yet the people persisted, and so God finally relented and the people were given a king.

Once the monarchy was established, charismatic individuals called prophets rose up to remind the people that, despite the fact that they had a human monarch, God was their true sovereign. These prophets insisted that the people were still bound to responsibilities they had agreed upon when they entered into covenant with God. These responsibilities required that they develop ways of offering due homage to God alone while at the same time maintaining an equitable manner of dealing with one another. Too often they failed to do so, and too often the monarchs failed to call them back to fidelity. Instead, many chose to exploit the products of Earth, resulting in the impoverishment of the vulnerable rather than mutual custodianship. Or they dallied with some of the Canaanite gods, placing their confidence in the fertility of the land rather than in the God who gave that fertility. This chapter looks at how a handful of prophets, grounded in values of the covenant, insisted that the intrinsic value of Earth be respected, that its fruits be shared by all, and that the dynamic powers of fertility be acknowledged as being under the control of God and God alone.

Literary Context

Prophetic voices move in and out of the story of ancient Israel. Some of them addressed the bureaucrats who made up the monarchy; others spoke directly to the citizens of the land. The first important voice was that of Samuel. He is sometimes referred to as the kingmaker, for it was Samuel who anointed both Saul (1 Sam 10:1) and David (1 Sam 16:13). Later, the prophet Nathan served in the court of David (2 Sam 7:1–17). He might also be considered a kingmaker, for he was instrumental in ensuring that David appointed his son Solomon to succeed him (1 Kgs 1:11–40). Elijah and his successor Elisha were formidable goads in the sides of northern kings, because they sought to abolish the idolatrous worship of Canaanite gods as it was practiced by many in that land.

There were other prophets besides Samuel, Nathan, Elijah, and Elisha who wielded significant political power. For example, the prophet Huldah confirmed the authenticity of a book of the law found in the Temple. She also prophesied the destruction of the Temple in Jerusalem and the manner of the death of the reigning king (2 Kgs 22:3–20). The proclamations or oracles of many of the prophets were remembered and later preserved in writing by their followers. Among them were men like Amos and Hosea, who continued in the footsteps of Elijah and Elisha, condemning some of the societal and cultic abuses that took place in the north. After the northern kingdom of Israel was defeated by the Assyrians (722 BCE), the southern kingdom repeatedly faced a similar fate. In view of this danger, Isaiah offered counsel to four consecutive southern monarchs. About 150 years later, Jeremiah warned the monarchy of his day that defeat by the Babylonians was imminent. Ezekiel later envisaged the ruin of the city of Jerusalem and the exile of the nation's religious and political leaders. Following the exile Daniel offered the vanquished people a vision of hope for the future. The oracles of those referred to as minor prophets usually focused on a single issue such as the rebuilding of the Temple (Haggai) or condemnation of the negligence of the priests (Malachi). Prophets such as these acted as the conscience of the nation.

Contrary to some popular understanding, the prophets did not speak only words of condemnation. Their messages always addressed the pressing needs of the time. When the people faced grave danger or were in desperate straits, prophets spoke words of encouragement and hope. Whenever success or prosperity led the people away from dependence on God or concern for the less fortunate among them, the prophetic message was one of denunciation. The passages examined here focus on the exploitation of the fruitfulness of the land and the attempt to control its powers of fertility.

Milk and Honey as Temptation

The wealth of Earth, whether the fertility that both produces living beings and provides sustenance for them or the rich mineral deposits within the ground, was considered a blessing from God. However, when that blessing experienced in the past or enjoyed in the present failed to instill trust that God would provide for the people in the future, or when greed or disregard for others prompted the powerful to take advantage of those who were less fortunate, then the wealth given freely as a blessing could only be seen as a temptation. Stories found in the Elijah cycle of narratives illustrate the people's betrayal in this regard and the need for a prophet to call them back to fidelity.

At the time of King Ahab (ca. 869–850 BCE), the land was experiencing a severe drought. The fickle people of Israel could not decide whether they should seek relief from the gods of the Canaanites or from the God of Israel. Of all the Canaanite gods mentioned in the Bible, Baal seems to have been the one that most troubled the prophets. The name Baal means "owner, ruler, or lord." In some passages the word simply refers to a Canaanite god (Judg 2:11; 3:7; 8:33; 10:6, 10). But usually it denotes a very specific deity, namely, Baal, son of the Canaanite high god, El. It is with this meaning that the word is used here. In Canaanite mythology Baal was a weather god associated with storms. The fact that rain refreshed the dry land and enabled growth to flourish led people to believe that Baal actually impregnated Earth. This explains why he was also considered a fertility deity, and why he posed a threat to the Israelites.

At this time of indecision on the part of the Israelites, the prophet Elijah boldly stepped forward:

> Elijah then came near to all the people, and said, "How long will you go limping with two different opinions? If the LORD is God, follow him; but if Baal, then follow him." (1 Kgs 18:21)

Elijah then challenged the prophets of Baal to a contest to see which deity was really ruler over the forces of nature. Taunting the other prophets, he pressed them to call down fire from heaven to consume two young bulls to be offered as sacrifice. The prophets of Baal were unsuccessful. Elijah prayed to the God of Israel, and a fire fell from heaven and consumed the offering. This was followed by a heavy rain that relieved the drought. Only then did the people acknowledge that the God of Israel had power over the forces of nature (1 Kgs 18:21–39).

The contest between the prophets of Baal and the prophet Elijah was really a contest between Baal and the God of Israel. Baal was not only considered the god of the Canaanites and the lord of that land, but, as already stated, he was also thought to be a storm deity responsible for fertility. The God of Israel was seen as a newcomer to the land, a minor military deity who delivered an insignificant people from oppression in Egypt. Thus Baal would be expected to provide the desperately needed rain. This story shows that the opposite was true. It is the God of Israel who rules the forces of nature, who brings the drought-ridden land back to life. Many of these stories are understood less as accurate accounts of historical events than as theological testimonies meant to reinforce the faith of the people. The people from whom these traditions originated would have understood the stories in this way.

A second narrative, already mentioned in Chapter 2, recounts King Ahab's desire to purchase a plot of land belonging to an Israelite named Naboth (1 Kgs 21). Since this was ancestral land, which by law was to be kept in Naboth's family or tribe, he refused the king's offer. Jezebel, the king's Phoenician wife, devised a fraudulent accusation that deprived Naboth of the land and ultimately sentenced him to death. The king then confiscated the land. Thus the monarchy, which was responsible for safeguarding the rights of the vulnerable, descended into conniving and land grabbing.

In both of these stories Jezebel played a leading role. In the first instance she supported the prophets of Baal in the contest with Elijah, and she sought to suppress the worship of the God of Israel; in the second she scorned the land directives of Israel and instigated the deceitful scheme that secured for the monarchy the land that Ahab coveted. Jezebel acted in ways meant to enhance the status of the monarchy, ways that were reprehensible according to the covenant laws of Israel but probably acceptable in her own Canaanite culture. In a sense she epitomizes the evils of Canaanite culture, evils that could lead the people away from the manner of living to which they had committed themselves, evils against which Israel would always have to guard itself.

A Dresser of Sycamore Trees

Amos, a man from the southern kingdom who prophesied in the north around 786–746 BCE, was neither a professional court prophet nor one who functioned at a shrine. He was a man of Earth:

> Then Amos answered Amaziah, "I am no prophet, nor a prophet's son; but I am a herdsman, and a dresser of syca-more trees." (Amos 7:14)

He knew what it was to be directly dependent on both soil composition and climate. His familiarity with the abundant yield that sprang up when nature was in balance provided him with insights into the damage that resulted from its imbalance. Economically, Amos was far from impoverished. However, to the well-to-do and indulgent people in the north who heard him at their shrine at Bethel, this rugged outdoorsman from the south must have seemed deprived, even primitive. This was a time of great prosperity for the northern kingdom, but not all of the citizenry enjoyed material comfort. It was to the abuses born of economic inequity that this prophet spoke.

"Thus says the Lord"

Upon his arrival in the north, Amos condemned the nations that surrounded this kingdom. He employed a poetic form of speech long associated with the Wisdom tradition: "Three things are stately . . . four are stately . . ." (see Prov 30:29–30). While the Wisdom tradition used this form to describe similarities, Amos uses it to condemn abuses.

The first condemnation was directed against Aram, the capital of Damascus and a powerful enemy to the north (Amos 1:3–5). This nation was accused of frequently taking advantage of the area known as Gilead, territory that at the time of allotment had been assigned to the northern tribes of Reuben and Gad (Josh 12:5). Gilead was a major trade route that crossed through Transjordan from Damascus in the north to the Gulf of Aqaba in the south. Damascus not only seized control of this trade route but treated the people of Gilead brutally. The people of Israel who heard this condemnation would have been pleased with the words of the prophet.

Amos next denounced Gaza, the capital of Philistia (Amos 1:6–8). This Mediterranean port city was located on another important north-south trade route. It too was condemned for its inhumane treatment of the women and children who were taken captive and sold to other nations. Tyre, the capital of Phoenicia, had gained its prominence from trade. Like Philistia, Tyre took people captive and sold them to Edom (Amos 1:9–10). Its sin may have been more heinous than that of Philistia, because there seems to have been an agreement between Tyre and the Israelites (see 1 Kgs 9:13). Gaining wealth and prominence through the trade of the goods of Earth led Damascus, Gaza, and Tyre to treat other less powerful people with disdain and cruelty. The bounty of Earth, which was meant to be enjoyed by all people, became, for these sinful nations, possessions that fed their greed and were used to keep others subservient.

The remaining nations all had ethnic links with Israel. The first was Edom, one of Israel's fiercest enemies throughout most of its history. It is here condemned for having "pursued his brother with a sword" (Amos 1:11–12). This brotherly enmity is reflected in the initial struggle between Jacob (Israel; Gen 35:10) and Esau (Edom; Gen 25:30). Furthermore, the condemnation of Philistia and Phoenicia states that they sold conquered people to Edom, in this way reinforcing Edom's loathsome reputation. Ammon and Moab trace their ancestry back to the daughters of Lot (Gen 19:36–38). According to Amos, Ammon's sin is barbaric (Amos 1:13–15). As a tactic in border warfare these people ripped open the bellies of pregnant women in an effort to thwart any possibility of a future generation for their enemies. Moab had a second ethnic tie to Israel through Ruth, the Moabite ancestress of David (Ruth 2:2). These people were considered despicable because they desecrated corpses (Amos 2:1–3). Finally, Amos denounced Judah (Amos 2:4–5), the kingdom from which the people in the north had separated themselves (1 Kgs 12:16). The sins of the other nations were social or moral failings. The sins of Judah were seen as violations of the covenant agreement made with God.

The condemnation of the nations that surrounded the northern kingdom of Israel must have been seen as good news to those who heard the prophet's searing words. These were, after all, people who had been Israel's rivals, people with whom they had been vying for power and prestige, people who threatened their security and their comfort. To hear a prophet of God revile these people and predict dire punishment for their depraved behavior must have cheered those who had gathered at the northern shrine at Bethel. This would have been particularly true regarding the condemnation of Judah, for the people in the north blamed the overbearing taxation of the Judean King Solomon for their break with his kingdom. A southern prophet's denunciation of his own nation was vindication for those in the north. Little did they know that Amos would next turn on them, rebuke them, and predict a grim fate for them as well. They must have stood aghast when the prophet pronounced against them the longest and most bitter denunciation.

Although several of the bordering nations denounced by Amos were known for their prominence in trading, they were not explicitly criticized for any commercial oppression. They were guilty of the brutality that accompanied their domination of others. The sins of Israel that Amos condemns were instances of the injustice perpetrated within the covenant community itself;[1] this was Israelite against Israelite:

> They sell the righteous for silver,
>   and the needy for a pair of sandals—
> they who trample the head of the poor into the
>   dust of the earth,
>   and push the afflicted out of the way.
>   (Amos 2:6–7)

Selling the poor is an example of the severity of debt slavery, a practice that was considered legal in many nations. It penalized debtors who were already poor and had no means to pay their creditors and no family members able to step forward to pay the debt. These debts could have been significant, hence the reference to silver, or they could have been as trifling as the price of a pair of sandals. Such debt was often a legal matter, and so judges were also involved in many of these oppressive decisions. Thus the legal system, which was meant to be a safeguard for those who were powerless and in financial straits, worked against them in favor of those with means and power. This was clearly a violation of the covenant prescription:

> If you lend money to my people, to the poor among you, you shall not deal with them as a creditor; you shall not exact interest from them. (Exod 22:25)

Not only did the wealthy consider payment of debt more important than concern for their less fortunate covenant partners, but they exercised the power that they possessed to further

---

[1] For another treatment of the relationship between Earth justice and human justice see David Jobling and Nathan Loewen, "Sketches for Earth Readings of the Book of Amos," in *The Earth Bible*, vol. 1, *Readings from the Perspective of Earth*, ed. Norman C. Habel (Cleveland: Pilgrim Press, 2000), 72–85.

trample the head of the poor into the dust of
the earth
and push the afflicted out of the way.
(Amos 2:7)

The Hebrew word in this passage translated "afflicted" is
anawim. The primary meaning of the verb from which this word
is derived is "to try to force submission, to afflict pain upon."
When used as an adjective or a noun the word stresses the condition of humility, which is the intended outcome of affliction.
This humility soon took on a spiritual meaning, focusing on an
attitude of neediness that results in total dependence on God.
Eventually, *anawim* was used almost exclusively in this spiritual
fashion. However, in Amos the reference is to actual economic
disadvantage.

The exceptional good fortune of the people in the northern
kingdom demonstrates how the "milk and honey," or abundance of the fruits of Earth, can become a serious temptation.
The luxurious lifestyle that many had fashioned for themselves
blinded them to the needs of the others in their company. Even
worse, their inordinate wealth gave them power, and this power
enabled them to dominate others less fortunate. Their total disdain for social justice is clear from the prophet's denunciation.
Such practices only produced more wealth and power. While this
was an obvious case of violation of their covenant responsibility
toward other covenant partners, it was much more. Economic
inequity and the oppression of others sprang from their disregard
for ecojustice. As defined here, ecojustice is the balance within
and among the powers of Earth. Since every aspect of human
existence is somehow grounded in the natural world, social injustice that results from an inequitable distribution of goods is
fundamentally an example of eco-injustice.

"I will not revoke the punishment"

After accusing the people of the north of flagrant disregard for
economic equity and societal harmony, the prophet announces
the consequences of such behavior. As is the case in so many
biblical passages, the texts imply or explicitly state that God
intervenes and punishes the erring people and frequently effects

this punishment through some dimension of natural creation. The day of the Lord, the day they looked forward to as a time of judgment on their enemies, will be a day of judgment for them (Amos 5:18–20). Finally, they will be ripped from the land that has been so generous to them, the land that had been allotted by God to their ancestors, and they will be taken as exiles into a foreign land (Amos 6:7). The gift of land that was freely given to them will eventually be taken away.

By means of five symbolic visions God shows Amos how the land, which was meant to be a blessing but now has become a temptation for the people, will actually be the source of their punishment. The first vision (Amos 7:1–3) threatens a destructive swarm of locusts. This would have recalled for them a similar swarm that acted as a plague for the Egyptians at the time of the Exodus, but from which their ancestors were spared (Exod 10:4–6). There would be no sparing there. The point is made that the locusts will appear at the time of the late growth of the crops. This would have been during our months of March and April, the time of the late spring rains. The harvest affected would be vegetables, not grain. Late spring was also the time when the early sowing of grain would begin to sprout. At this time of year a plague of locusts would wipe out both the fully grown vegetable crop and the sprouting grain crop. This would affect two harvests, and the results would be disastrous.

Amos's task as prophet was twofold. First, he was charged to deliver the word of the LORD to the people, regardless of how searing that word might be. Second, he was to act as advocate for the people before God. This second responsibility could be as burdensome as the first, for he had to plead the cause of an unfaithful people. Nonetheless, he did so:

> "O LORD God, forgive, I beg you!" (Amos 7:2)

and

> The LORD relented concerning this. (Amos 7:3)

In the second symbolic vision (Amos 7:4–6), a raging fire rains down and consumes the fields. This fire not only devours the land, but it also dries up the "great deep" (v. 4), the subterranean waters that lie beneath Earth and feed the rivers, springs, and lakes. Thus, not only is the present crop destroyed, but the supply of rejuvenating water is depleted as well. Drought and famine threaten any future life. Once again Amos pleads for the people:

> "O LORD God, cease, I beg you!" (Amos 7:5)

and once again

> The LORD relented concerning this. (Amos
> 7:6)

The third vision (Amos 7:7–9) is difficult to understand, primarily because the key Hebrew word cannot be easily translated. It appears nowhere else in the entire Bible, and so there is no other context that might help us discover its meaning. The long-standing translation—"plumb line"—was decided upon because of the word's similarity to an Akkadian word. This rendering suggests that a plumb line used to measure the perpendicular character of a wall be used to measure the uprightness of the people. Since they do not "measure up," the line's straightness exposes their crookedness. A second possible translation ("tin") points to the instability of a building made of tin. In this version tin would underscore the instability of the people. Whichever translation is preferred, the basic meaning of the vision is clear, namely, that God has taken stock of the people and they have been found wanting. Following this vision the prophet does not plead their cause, and God does not relent. Instead, the Lord declares, "I will never again pass them by" (Amos 7:8), a reference to God's "passing over" their ancestors as he punished their oppressors at the time of their deliverance from Egyptian bondage.

The late-summer basket of fruit of the fourth vision (Amos 8:1–2) represents the ultimate harvest time. Its significance can be derived from the words of the Lord that follow:

> "The end has come upon my people Israel;
>   I will never again pass them by." (Amos
> 8:2)

The third and fourth visions include the same divine condemnation: There will be no reprieve; the people must face their punishment. God insists: "Surely, I will never forget any of their deeds" (Amos 8:7). What have they done? Their greed for more of the treasures of Earth has resulted in the oppression of the less fortunate among them, even to the extent of perverting monthly celebrations and the holiness of the sabbath:

> Hear this, you that trample on the needy,
>   and bring to ruin the poor of the land,
>   saying,
> "When will the new moon be over
>   so that we may sell grain;
> and the sabbath,
>   so that we may offer wheat for sale?"
>   (Amos 8:4–5a)

The people will have to endure the consequences of their sinfulness:

> Shall not the land tremble on this account,
>   and everyone mourn who lives in it,
> and all of it rise like the Nile,
>   and be tossed about and sink again,
> like the Nile of Egypt?
>   On that day, says the Lord GOD,
> I will make the sun go down at noon,
>   and darken the earth in broad daylight.
> I will turn your feasts into mourning,
>   and all your songs into lamentation;
> I will bring sackcloth on all loins,
>   and baldness on every head;
> I will make it like the mourning
>   for an only son,
> and the end of it like a bitter day.
> (Amos 8:8–10)

While the fourth vision simply announces the suffering the people will face, the fifth vision describes that suffering in graphic detail (Amos 9). There will be no place to hide, neither Sheol (the place of the dead), nor the heavens (the limits of the universe where God reigns supreme), nor the top of Mount Carmel (a high mountain in the northeast part of the land), nor the bottom of the sea (the lowest part of the known world). As strange as it might sound, not even captivity by another nation in another land will provide an escape from the consequences their disloyalty has brought upon them.

As is the case in so many biblical passages, the texts imply or explicitly state that God intervenes and punishes the erring people and frequently effects this punishment through some dimension of natural creation. However, there are other passages that suggest that the prophet understands that some of the trials that the people face are more the consequences of unavoidable cause and effect:

> Do two walk together
>   unless they have made an appointment?
> Does a lion roar in the forest,
>   when it has no prey?
> Does a young lion cry out from its den,
>   if it has caught nothing?
> Does a bird fall into a snare on the earth,
>   when there is no trap for it?
> Does a snare spring up from the ground,
>   when it has taken nothing?
> Is a trumpet blown in a city,
>   and the people are not afraid? (Amos
>   3:3–6)

All of these examples are drawn from common experience and are meant to remind the people that there is order in the world and that nothing is really accidental. Life and experience demonstrate the interconnectedness within all of natural creation. The early Israelites may not have understood some of the hardships they faced as natural consequences of their behavior, but contemporary readers can. The latter know that there is indeed order in the natural world. They also know that through foolish or greedy behavior people can disrupt that delicate balance of nature, and if they do, they will suffer the consequences of that imbalance.

Furthermore, a luxurious lifestyle at the expense of other people can cause threatening social unrest and consequently turn that comfort upside down. Amos's warning still applies:

> Therefore because you trample on the poor
>   and take from them levies of grain,
> you have built houses of hewn stone,
>   but you shall not live in them;
> you have planted pleasant vineyards,
>   but you shall not drink their wine. (Amos
>   5:11)

In many instances there is no way to rehabilitate passages that depict God using components of the natural world as instruments of punishment.[2] Such passages deny the intrinsic value of creation; they also portray God in a very negative light. All one can do is recognize that such descriptions and portrayals are characteristics of a culture that does not yet enjoy the scientific insight of today. Nonetheless, the fundamental meaning of such passages is little changed. They warn us that we cannot take lightly the natural balance enjoyed by the forces of nature. If we do, we make ourselves and our ecosystem vulnerable to both natural and social instability.

Most commentators maintain that the hopeful words found at the end of Amos's message (9:11–15) were written by a different hand, someone from the exilic or postexilic period. Regardless of the origin of this piece, the understanding of the relationship between and among the energies of nature is the same. Once God steps in and repairs the fractured covenant relationship, the imbalance within the powers of nature is corrected:

> The time is surely coming, says the LORD,
>   when the one who plows shall overtake
>   the one who reaps,

---

[2] Hilary Marlow argues that nature is not a passive instrument in the hand of a punishing God, but rather God's partner in the punishment of the sinful nation. See "The Other Prophet! The Voice of Earth in the Book of Amos," in *Exploring Ecological Hermeneutics*, ed. Norman C. Habel and Peter Trudinger, 75–83 (Atlanta: Society of Biblical Literature, 2008).

and the treader of grapes
the one who sows the seed;
the mountains shall drip sweet wine,
and all the hills shall flow with it. (Amos
9:13)

Earth will once again yield such bountiful produce that harvesting will not be finished before the land is made ready for the next crop, or the wine presser will not be finished with the first crop before a second is planted. Order will be reestablished and the fruits of that order will be abundant. The "land flowing with milk and honey" will once again be a blessing rather than a temptation.

The people at the time of the prophet might have thought that this return to prosperity would be affected by direct action of God. Today, scientifically astute readers understand this passage differently. They are aware of the marvelous and mysterious ability of Earth to repair and rejuvenate itself. Given time, Earth can come alive again; water can cleanse itself; air can rid itself of many pollutants. Such demythologizing in no way denies the power and action of God. Rather, it describes that power and action as working through nature, not despite it. However, if this rejuvenation is to happen, people must recapture an appreciation of the intrinsic value of Earth, acknowledge the interconnectedness and interdependence that exists between and among all Earth creatures, redirect human aspirations and plans so that they are aligned with the universe's dynamic design, and recommit themselves to a sense of custodianship with other members of the community of Earth. In other words, what is required is *metanoia*, a change of mind and heart.

A Broken Promise

The broken marriage relationship between the prophet Hosea and his wife, Gomer, is used as a metaphor to highlight the broken covenant relationship between God and the northern kingdom of Israel. Hosea and Amos seem to have been contemporaries, and both appear to have prophesied to the people of the north. However, there is no indication that the two prophets knew each other. Nor do they concentrate on the same abuses. Amos was primarily concerned with matters of social justice; Hosea, who delivered his message some time during the final decade of the existence of the northern kingdom (760–720 BCE), focused on the people's participation in Canaanite fertility rituals.

Today it is believed that only a small number of the people who eventually made up the twelve tribes could trace their ancestry back to those who had been delivered out of Egypt and entered the land under the leadership of Joshua. Most of the people were originally Canaanites already living in the land and worshiping traditional Canaanite deities. These people simply transferred their political allegiance to the newly formed tribal alliance that came to be known as the tribes of Jacob and their religious devotion to the God of that alliance. This would mean that at the time of Hosea, many of the people in the north had either returned to some of their former Canaanite practices or had never really purged themselves of them.

Amos had criticized the people for allowing the prosperity that they enjoyed to tempt them to greed and various forms of social inequity. Hosea cried out against their attempt to ensure continuation of this abundance through their participation in Canaanite fertility rituals, thus turning away from exclusive worship of their own God. This betrayal of the intimate covenant relationship with God parallels the infidelity of which Hosea accuses his own wife.

"They have played the whore"

The major deity of the Ancient Near East was the creator god El. His partner was the fertility goddess, Asherah, who gave birth to Baal. Though there are few references to El in the Old Testament, devotion to Asherah flourished among the northern tribes of Israel (1 Kgs 15:13; 18:19; 2 Kgs 21:7; 23:4–7). Worship of Baal was also a constant threat to fidelity to the God of Israel (1 Kgs 16:31–32; 18:19–40; 2 Kgs 10:18–28). In the pantheon of the gods Asherah was portrayed as both Baal's mother and his partner, and the sexual union of these two deities was believed to result in the fertility of Earth and all the living things that spring from Earth.[3] Those devoted to these deities believed that they could ensure fertility for themselves, their crops, and their herds if they participated in some form of fertility ritual. In order to accomplish this, they developed various forms of religious prostitution (1 Kgs 14:23–24). In the ritual a priest or a male member of the community represented Baal, and a priestess or female member of the community represented Asherah. The people believed that through ritualized sexual union they could control the forces of fertility.

The religion of Israel considered the fertility ritual abominable for several reasons. Most important, it was a departure from exclusive worship of the God of Israel, which was a fundamental element of Israel's faith. Second, it violated the intimate covenant relationship made between God and this people, a covenant to which the people had freely committed themselves. Third, it suggested that Baal and Asherah controlled the powers of life and fertility, not the God of Israel. Fourth, it was an attempt on the part of the people to appropriate these powers to themselves in order to manipulate them according to their own desires. Since the covenant relationship was seen as analogous to a marriage agreement, Hosea viewed the people's participation in fertility rites as adultery or whoring:

> For a spirit of whoredom has led them astray,
>   and they have played the whore, forsaking
>   their God.
> They sacrifice on the tops of the mountains,
>   and make offerings upon the hills,
> under oak, poplar, and terebinth,
>   because their shade is good.
> Therefore your daughters play the whore,
>   and your daughters-in-law commit adul-
>   tery. (Hos 4:12–13)

---

[3] For an intriguing treatment of Earth community, see Laurie B. Braaten, "Earth Community in Hosea 2," in *The Earth Bible*, vol. 4, *The Earth's Story in the Psalms and the Prophets*, ed. Norman C. Habel. 185–203 (Cleveland: Pilgrim Press, 2001).

Aspects of Hosea's dysfunctional family throw light on the deteriorated condition of the people's covenant relationship with God. First is his relationship with his wife Gomer:

> "Go, take for yourself a wife of whoredom and have children of whoredom, for the land commits great whoredom by forsaking the LORD." (Hos 1:2)

Some interpreters maintain that Gomer was a cult prostitute. Others believe that she was guilty of violating one or more of the customs that determined how women were to behave in ancient Israelite society. If a woman refused to conform to even the least important of these customs, she brought shame on the men of her family. Whatever Gomer's situation might have been, she acted inappropriately and thus challenged the marital relationship she had with Hosea. Following this depiction of Gomer, the names of their three children are telling. The first son was called Jezreel, the name of the valley where in the future a battle would be fought that would bring an end to the northern kingdom (Hos 1:4–5); Lo-ruhamah, the daughter's name, means "not pitied" (v. 6) and announces God's attitude toward the people because of their sinfulness; the second son was called Lo-ammi, "not my people" (v. 8), meaning that the people's choice to worship another deity threatened their very status as God's chosen people.

Hosea is not slow to condemn Gomer:

> For their mother has played the whore;
> > she who conceived them has acted shame-
> > > fully.
> For she said, "I will go after my lovers;
> > they give me my bread and my water,
> > my wool and my flax, my oil and my
> > > drink." (Hos 2:5)

It seems that the only way the people would come to realize that it was the God of Israel who controls the forces of life and fertility and not Baal was to take away the fertility of this "land flowing with milk and honey," and so God declares:

> She did not know
>> that it was I who gave her the grain,
>> the wine, and the oil,
> and who lavished upon her silver
>> and gold that they used for Baal.
> Therefore I will take back my grain in its time,
>> and my wine in its season;
> and I will take away my wool and my flax,
>> which were to cover her nakedness. (Hos
>> 2:8–9)

> I will lay waste her vines and her fig trees,
>> of which she said,
> "These are my pay,
>> which my lovers have given me."
> I will make them a forest,
>> and the wild animals shall devour them.
>> (Hos 2:12)

The torment that Gomer, and analogously Israel, will suffer should not be seen as simply vindictive or retributive on God's part. It is meant to demonstrate in a forceful manner that the God of Israel is the authentic source of fertility. Since the land and its abundance were freely given by God, God can rightfully take it back. How this will happen is not stated.

"How can I give you up?"

The marriage metaphor with its sense of personal commitment highlights the intimate character of the covenant relationship. Hosea's experience of personal betrayal engendered grief, not merely anger. The metaphor suggests a comparable sentiment in God. This is most unusual, for people of the Ancient Near East viewed their deities as powerful potentates, incapable of being hurt by mere mortals. Yet, this is precisely the image of God that is revealed in Hosea's words:

> When Israel was a child, I loved him,
>> and out of Egypt I called my son.
> The more I called them,

the more they went from me;
they kept sacrificing to the Baals,
    and offering incense to idols.
Yet it was I who taught Ephraim to walk,
    I took them up in my arms;
        but they did not know that I healed them.
I led them with cords of human kindness,
    with bands of love.
I was to them like those
    who lift infants to their cheeks.
        I bent down to them and fed them. (Hos
        11:1–4)

A divine tenderness is revealed in these words, a tenderness that will not be deterred by the betrayal of the one so deeply loved, yet so unfaithful to that love. The metaphor changes as God is depicted here as a loving mother who gently cares for and embraces a wayward son. Not even wanton rebelliousness can undo God's motherly love.

God's willingness to begin anew with this people is seen in the promise of a new day, a day when the covenant relationship will be renewed and all creation will experience a return to its natural balance:

On that day I will answer, says the LORD,
    I will answer the heavens
    and they shall answer the earth;
and the earth shall answer the grain, the wine,
        and the oil,
    and they shall answer Jezreel;
    and I will sow him for myself in the land.
And I will have pity on *Lo-ruhamah*,
    and I will say to *Lo-ammi*, "You are my
        people";
    and he shall say, "You are my God." (Hos
    2:21–23)

On that day, the names of the prophet's children will no longer signify destruction or rejection. Instead, the devastated Jezreel will once again be fertile; *Lo-ruhamah* (not pitied) will once again know divine pity; *Lo ammi* (not my people) will return to being God's chosen people. Furthermore, the land of grain and wine and oil will once more be a "land flowing with milk and honey."

If misfortune is not to be understood as divine punishment for misconduct, then good fortune should not be considered reward for good behavior. That is not to say that natural abundance is not a blessing from God. It is blessing; but it is not reward. We receive good things from God because God is good, not because we are.

The image of God sketched in the passage above conforms to ancient Israel's concept of God as one who punishes and rewards, a concept that is actually quite limiting. Rather than depicting God as free, it presents divine action as determined by human behavior. When human beings are sinful, God punishes; when they are faithful, God rewards. However, this is not the only image of God that Hosea offers us. We have seen that God is also depicted as a tender mother, who cares for her son even when he is rebellious (Hos 11:1–4). This apparent discrepancy reminds us that no image or description can capture the essence of the mighty God. While each characterization expresses some divine feature, if it stands by itself without modification it is a distortion.

The messages of the prophets Amos and Hosea show that the people to whom they preached had lost an appreciation for the intrinsic value of the riches of Earth. They were only interested in the comfort and pleasure that they could derive from them, or the ability to ensure that they would always have these riches at their disposal. They lacked a sense of custodianship or responsibility for the care of Earth. Since neither Earth nor the poor of Earth could cry out against such exploitation, the prophets became the voice of both the disadvantaged people and the ravaged Earth.

Blessing or Temptation?

The extravagant abundance with which Earth's table is laid is meant to be a blessing from God for all. However, human frailty has often turned this blessing into a temptation that feeds human greed. People have amassed goods, thinking that these treasures will diminish their vulnerability and compensate for their sense of insecurity and inadequacy in the face of the contingencies of life. They do not see themselves as part of the wonders of Earth, but as titleholders and unrestricted authorities over all. Such an attitude presumes that Earth's wealth is meant primarily, even exclusively, for human enhancement. It rejects, if it even considers, the intrinsic value of Earth and all that comes from Earth.

Wealth can also give some people undue power over others. It can set up a false hierarchy of importance, giving the privileged more voice in making decisions for the entire group. Material deprivation often diminishes a person's sense of self-worth, thus reinforcing the presumed importance of the powerful. Such social imbalance is spawned by disregard for the mutual custodianship of Earth and Earth's riches. The riches of Earth are meant for all people, not merely for a few.

The prophetic message of the prophet Amos is as relevant today as it was in the eighth century BCE. It can be easily retrieved and interpreted today with very little difficulty. Millions of people today languish in poverty while others accrue more wealth than they would be able to enjoy in several lifetimes. Major economic systems depend on our ability to consume what we do not need or may not be able to afford. In such systems, goods have become more important than people. An appreciation of the community of Earth has been lost, and those who *have* seem unaware of their responsibility to and for those who *have not*. However, the voice of the poor is really the voice of Earth crying out for a just distribution of its riches. In a very real sense economic injustice is an aspect of eco-injustice.

The riches of Earth have become a temptation in yet another way. Recognizing the wondrous energies of Earth and the remarkable abilities of human beings to understand and manage those energies, some maintain that these human abilities are limitless. This attitude even leads them to question the existence of a sovereign creator. Ancient Israel's desire to ensure and control fertility of land and herds and human reproduction is not far removed from the modern attempt to control the energies of the universe. The fertility cults that the prophet Hosea condemned may seem quite naive to us today. This does not mean that the message of this prophet has lost its religious force. On the contrary. It can be retrieved and interpreted for people today. This is because the desire to control the forces of life, whether human life or life in any of its myriad forms, is with us still. Consequently, this prophet's message is as important today as it was in the past.

This is not to say that we should refrain from seeking to discover ways of enhancing life. Our yearning to understand is a gift from God, as is our facility in scientific development. This fact notwithstanding, there is a very thin line between straining to understand the marvels of the universe of which we are a part and presuming that we are in control of those marvels. We are constantly learning about our vast universe, discovering its majesty and power, evolving as the entire universe evolves, moving as part of it to more and more convergence. Still, we are fragile creatures, dependent on the whole for our existence. Though the mysteries of this universe will probably always pose some form of temptation for us, we will be able to deal appropriately with those mysteries if we are conscious of and attentive to relevant ecojustice principles.

"Where shall wisdom be found?"

—Job 28:12

Chapter Four

Even a cursory look at ancient Israel's national story reveals the people's conviction that God was active in their history. They believed that God had chosen them, guided them, revealed the Law to them, and rewarded and punished them according to their fidelity to that Law. In fact, God was perceived as the principal actor in the drama of their history.

Despite the importance of this story, other biblical literature provides a quite different perspective. Reflection on life and observation of nature led the sages to conclude that there is a kind of order inherent in creation. They believed that if they could discern how this order operated and harmonize their lives in accord with it, they would live peacefully and fruitfully. Conversely, failure to identify and conform to this order would result in frustration, misfortune, and misery. This second biblical perspective is known as Wisdom.

Wisdom, as understood by the ancient Israelites, dealt with general questions of human welfare, human value, and human destiny. Reflecting on the consequences of behavior, the people concluded that whatever benefited humankind was a good to be pursued and whatever was injurious should be avoided and condemned. The success and the happiness that certain behavior brought set the standard for any course of action. Success was also considered concrete evidence of the wisdom and righteousness of the person who succeeded.

The Wisdom tradition poses a paradox for the ecosensitive reader. On the one hand, it is based on the conviction that there is order in the natural world and that success and happiness depend upon one's willingness and ability to live in harmony with that order. Such an understanding of universal natural laws bears a resemblance to the ecojustice principle of interconnectedness. However, the primary focus of Wisdom teaching is human fulfillment, and everything else serves that purpose. To the extent that such fulfillment is advanced as the exclusive goal of life, this perspective is clearly anthropocentric. In this chapter various passages from the Wisdom tradition are examined in order to look anew at natural creation and the role that human beings play in creation.

Literary Context

The Wisdom literature of the Bible includes Job, Proverbs, and Ecclesiastes, as well as the deutero-canonical or apocryphal Wisdom of Solomon and Ecclesiasticus. Several psalms are classified as Wisdom psalms (Pss 1, 37, 49, 73, 91, 112, 119, 127, 128, 133, 139).[1] Since the primary function of the Wisdom tradition is instruction in a style of living that will ensure well-being and prosperity, its emphasis is on education and training. Thus, the literary forms found in this tradition function pedagogically. Such forms include proverbs that describe particular life situations for the purpose of encouraging appropriate behavior; parables, riddles, and questions that tease the mind and lead to new insights; and stories that have a moral to teach.

Most of the material in these books is poetic in form. Unlike standard classical or contemporary poetry, there is virtually no rhyme, and the rhythm follows tonal patterns that are usually lost when the original Hebrew is translated. One characteristic that is identifiable even in translation is the correspondence of thought in successive half lines. In this feature, known as parallelism, the thought in the first line is repeated in what follows:

> At the busiest corner   she cries out;
> At the entrance of the city gates   she speaks.
> (Prov 1:21)

---

[1] Some commentators consider the Song of Songs a Wisdom book.

or contrasted:

A wise child makes	a glad father,
But a foolish child is	a mother's grief.
	(Prov 10:1)

or developed:

> A capable wife who can find?
> She is far more precious than jewels. (Prov
> 31:10)

The fundamental theological focus of this tradition is retribution, which teaches that goodness is rewarded and misbehavior is punished. Or to use the language of the Wisdom tradition: wise action brings happiness and foolishness results in grief. This theme undergirds each of the Wisdom books: Proverbs, Wisdom of Solomon, and Ecclesiasticus are collections of maxims that offer advice for a manner of living that will result in happiness; Job recounts the struggles of a righteous man who sees no justice in his suffering; Ecclesiastes challenges a superficial understanding of success and advocates finding happiness in the life one has been given; the Wisdom psalms describe consequences of both wise and foolish behavior.

The ancient Israelites believed that there is a fundamental and universal set of laws that govern the entire universe. Thus, aspects of the created world enjoy a prominent place in the teaching of the sages. However, many commentators argue that since human fulfillment is the primary focus of this teaching, the natural world is important only to the extent that it throws light on human needs, goals, or accomplishments. For them, creation is only prized for its usefulness, not for its intrinsic value. A closer reading of some passages in this tradition will uncover the possibility of a more ecosensitive reading.

"They will teach you"

The Wisdom tradition has been variously described as a humanistic outlook on life; a worldview for coping with reality; a search for the underlying principles of causality and order for the purpose of conforming to them; and an attempt to organize an otherwise chaotic existence. Each of these characterizations, though distinctly nuanced, highlights the primary concern of the movement, namely, fashioning character in human beings in order to ensure successful living.

Regardless of how this tradition is characterized, all commentators agree that wisdom can only be achieved through diligent reflection on and learning from experience. A somewhat enigmatic proverb states this quite emphatically:

> The beginning of wisdom is this: Get wisdom,
> And whatever else you get, get insight.
>   (Prov 4:7)

While this proverb offers straightforward advice, it fails to provide direction for how it might be accomplished. An old adage offers a bit of insight: Experience is the best teacher. This implies that experience brings wisdom. While there certainly is truth in this statement, we all know that experience alone does not guarantee wisdom. In fact, there is another adage that suggests otherwise: There's no fool like an old fool. This statement insists that age and the experience accrued through it guarantee age and experience and nothing more. Wisdom comes when one learns from that experience. Still, the importance of experience in acquiring wisdom cannot be overestimated. In fact, contrary to what the first adage states, experience is not the best teacher, it is the only teacher. Whatever we know, we have learned from experience, either our own or the experience of others. Traditions and customs, whether political, social, or religious, develop from the insights gained from the experience of members of the group and are handed down generation after generation. A truly wise person learns from reflection on both personal and traditional experience.

An interesting passage found in the Book of Job points to a specific way of learning from experience:

> But ask the animals, and they will teach you;
>   the birds of the air, and they will tell you;

> ask the plants of the earth, and they will teach
> you;
> and the fish of the sea will declare to you.
> (Job 12:7–8)

In this passage, Job claims that the animals know that God is responsible for the suffering that he, Job, is enduring. In other words, the natural world has something to teach human beings.[2] Learning from animals is further explained in a passage found in Proverbs. There we read that the ant, known for its diligence in working, has something to teach lazy human beings:

> Go to the ant, you lazybones;
> Consider its ways and be wise.
> Without having any chief
> Or officer or ruler,
> It prepares its food in summer,
> And gathers its sustenance in harvest. (Prov
> 6:6–8)

Observing the behavior of various animals, the sages gained insights into the habits of these animals and concluded that the natural world follows various laws. They believed that human society is governed by similar laws. They further held that the animals' success in accomplishing the goals set for them by these laws could be used as impetus for encouraging corresponding appropriate human behavior. The animals do indeed have something to teach human creatures.

The kind of metaphoric expression found in these passages is very common in traditional societies. Unfortunately, contemporary readers too often understand metaphors such as these as little more than creative embellishments, artistic flourishes intended to create a certain rhetorical effect. They fail to realize that metaphor was an integral component of the ancient Israelite world of understanding. It communicated a way of both seeing

---

[2] This was a very common point of view and is still held by traditional societies even today. *Aesop's Fables* is probably the most widely known example of this standpoint.

and thinking. Metaphorical language is not just expository or explanatory. It is artistic speech in which form and meaning are inseparable, in which the words "are more than the clothing . . . of the content."[3] Traditional societies think concretely in analogies, not abstractly in concepts, as most contemporary societies think. For them, metaphor is more than a figure of speech; it is a doorway through which they step into their own world of meaning.

The technique of learning from creation can be seen in the Book of Ecclesiastes as well. There, the sage calls on components of the natural world to teach a different lesson. The very first verses of the first chapter describe, but do not identify, the speaker of the book. In Hebrew he is called Qoheleth, the one who presides over the *qahal* (assembly). In translations from the Greek he is called Preacher or Ecclesiastes, an official of the *ekklesia* (assembly). This speaker is further identified as the son of David, king of Israel. No doubt the reference is to Solomon, the one esteemed in popular devotion as the wise man par excellence. This identification is probably not historically accurate, but rather served to give legitimacy to the teaching of the book, which was somewhat unorthodox.

A surface reading of this book has left many people today with the impression that Qoheleth was a skeptic, a cynic, even a hedonist. He did, after all, insist that "all is vanity," a "chase after the wind," and he advised his hearers to enjoy life. His view of life seems too pessimistic for some. Even today some readers question whether this book should be considered authentic Wisdom teaching. But an understanding of his teaching technique offers a more positive point of view.

Qoheleth sets out to discover the depths and the breadth of all human endeavors. He poses an encompassing and profound question:

> "What do people gain from all the toil
> At which they toil under the sun?" (Eccl 1:3)[4]

---

[3] Peter W. Macky, *The Centrality of Metaphors to Biblical Thought: A Method for Interpreting the Bible* (Lewiston, NY: The Edward Mellen Press, 1990), 273.

[4] This same question is posed in other places in the book (see Eccl 3:9; 5:11, 16).

What is the point of all the effort human beings put into their endeavors if nothing comes of it? Throughout his observations Qoheleth employs examples from nature to demonstrate the futility of much of human striving. The regularity within the natural world, employed in the Book of Proverbs to encourage social harmony (Prov 30:15–33), is characterized by Qoheleth as monotonous, lacking any sense of fulfillment:

> The sun rises and the sun goes down,
>> and hurries to the place where it rises.
> The wind blows to the south,
>> and goes around to the north;
> round and round goes the wind,
>> and on its circuits the wind returns.
> All streams run to the sea,
>> but the sea is not full;
> to the place where the streams flow,
>> there they continue to flow. (Eccl 1:5–7)

The sun adheres to the same cycles, the wind follows the same currents, and the rivers and streams empty into an insatiable sea. They simply repeat themselves without accomplishing anything. What does the sun achieve by rising and setting if it must repeat the cycle again and again with no variation and no advance? What profit comes from the wind's endless movement if it never arrives at any destination? To what avail do the streams quench the thirst of an insatiable sea? This sage urges his hearers to learn yet another lesson from nature. Human striving for gain is nothing but wearisome labor that must be repeated and repeated with no promise of completion and no assurance of gratification. This is what Qoheleth considers "vanity of vanities" or "a chase after the wind."

Despite the apparent cynicism of these phrases, Qoheleth does not really despair of life itself. It is something about the way life is lived by some that is "a chase after the wind." In the very beginning of the book he states that he has tested the extent to which pleasure or success can give ultimate satisfaction, and he found them wanting. Also, since death is the inevitable destiny of both the wise and the foolish, not even wisdom can guarantee definitive human fulfillment. Qoheleth does not disdain pleasure or success or the search for wisdom, but he calls those foolish who hope to be completely gratified by them. One might ask: Is this cynicism? Or realism?

Qoheleth draws on what he has observed of various components of the natural world to teach his hearers that there is no guarantee that a sense of fulfillment will accompany accomplishment of the tasks one undertakes in order to achieve that fulfillment. He then exhorts them to enjoy what they can with what they have at the moment, without hoping that real fulfillment will be had in the future:

> There is nothing better for mortals than to eat and drink, and find enjoyment in their toil. This also, I saw, is from the hand of God. (Sir 2:24)[5]

It is passages such as these that have led some to claim that Qoheleth is a hedonist, someone who believes that pleasure and happiness are the highest goal. This is far from the case, for Qoheleth insists that God wants human beings to live as fully as possible the life that God has given them. According to him, enjoyment is found in the very living of life: in eating, in drinking, in the work itself rather than in the sense of being sated or in the wealth that one might hope to gain by it. This pleasure, like everything else in life, has come from the hand of God and should be enjoyed.

Both Proverbs and Ecclesiastes show that the Wisdom teachers turned to nature to teach important lessons about life. Proverbs emphasized this natural order so that one might promote social order; Qoheleth turned his eye to the repetitive movements in nature to encourage living in the present moment. (We will see later that the author of Job also employs aspects of nature to teach Job.) Lest we think that nature is merely used as a tool to advance human learning, it is precisely the integrity of creation following its inherent nature that these sages call human beings to emulate. The ecojustice principle of intrinsic value undergirds this pedagogical technique.

The ancient Israelites might have interpreted this natural order in a mythological manner, but today's readers need not do so.

---

[5] See also Sir 3:13, 22; 5:19; 8:15; 9:9.

Contemporary science has brought us to see that we are indeed subject to many of the same laws of nature as are other members of the community of Earth. This resonates with the ecojustice principle of interconnectedness. Furthermore, this interconnectedness is more than metaphoric. Today, we know that physically we are connected in the very marrow of our bones. That the natural world has something to teach human beings might be seen as the principle that states that "Earth is a subject capable of raising its voice in celebration and against injustice."[6] These Wisdom teachers insist that the manner in which Earth and Earth creatures follow the laws that govern them leads human beings to insight into human life and experience.

"Things too wonderful for me"

Job is also taught by means of components from the natural world. In fact, it was a specific characteristic of the cosmos that ultimately resolved Job's dilemma. The story of Job is both straightforward and well known. It is the story of a righteous man who was stricken with catastrophic misfortune and struggled to understand why this had happened to him. The story itself is well crafted, and only an appreciation of the many levels of its artistry will enable the reader to appreciate the manner in which it unfolds. Several strands of theology are woven throughout the drama. Chief among them are retribution, which states that goodness will be rewarded and evil punished; theodicy or the vindication of the righteousness of God; and theological anthropology, a religious understanding of the nature of the human beings.

In the prose prologue of the Book of Job, the author takes great pains to present Job as a man of incontestable virtue. He is described as "blameless and upright, one who feared God and turned away from evil" (Job 1:1). God always refers to Job with these words (1:8; 2:3), thus giving legitimacy to the description. Next, Job's wealth, the external evidence of that righteousness, is itemized. According to the theory of retribution, if goodness

---

[6] Norman C. Habel, *The Earth Bible*, vol. 1, *Readings from the Perspective of Earth* (Cleveland: The Pilgrim Press, 2000), 24.

is rewarded, then extraordinary goodness will yield prolific good fortune. This is certainly the case with Job, who is said to be "the greatest of all the people in the east" (1:3). It is important to sketch this profile of Job as a man who is extravagantly wealthy because of his righteousness so that the impending unfathomable mystery of his misfortune can stand in stark contrast.

The real drama of the book unfolds in the poetic speeches of Job and the men who visit him. One after another, in three cycles of speeches, he complains while they claim various theological explanations of his predicament. Everything they say is informed by some aspect of the theology of retribution. Job argues that according to this theology, he is being unfairly treated. He insists that he does not deserve the hardships that are consuming him. Again and again he attests to his uprightness. If anyone is at fault, it is God, who has allowed this injustice to befall him. The visitors defend both their retributive evaluation of Job's situation and their understanding of the justice of God. They argue that God, whose righteousness is beyond reproach, would not allow such suffering if Job did not deserve it. According to them, to even question God's righteousness simply unmasks the depths of Job's sinfulness. While both Job and his visitors uphold the principles of retribution and divine justice, they are poles apart in recognizing the implications of these principles in this concrete situation.

Job and his visitors are at an impasse. It is then that Job calls upon God to step in and give evidence of Job's sinfulness, if such evidence even exists. God responds, but not in the way Job has demanded. The arguments between Job and his visitors have been over questions of justice. God never even broaches that topic. Some commentators criticize God for this, accusing God of being callous or disinterested. Such a reading fails to recognize the pedagogical technique of the Wisdom teacher, which is the practice of posing questions, not providing answers. It also fails to appreciate the importance of the content of these questions, which is some aspect of the natural world.

God finally breaks the cosmic silence and thunders through the heavens. Meteorological phenomena of this kind often accompanied a theophanic experience. Such phenomena were seen as manifestations of divine majesty and power. The God who answers Job by questioning him is the Creator God. There is a sardonic tone to the queries put to Job, for the questions all focus on Job's inability to understand or to control the forces or creatures of Earth:

> "Who is this . . . ?" (38:2)
> "Where were you . . . ?" (38:4)
> "Have you commanded . . . ?" (38:12)
> "Can you bind . . . ?" (38:31)
> "Can you lift up . . . ?" (38:34)
> "Can you send forth . . . ?" (38:35)
> "Do you know . . . ?" (39:1)
> "Can you number . . . ?" (39:2)
> "Can you tie . . . ?" (39:10)
> "Do you give . . . ?" (39:19)
> "Can you draw out . . . ?" (41:1)

Question after question is put to Job, each one challenging his knowledge of cosmic reality or his control over it. What does he know about the purpose or scheme of God in the creation, control, and maintenance of the world? All these questions confront Job with the limitations of his own creaturehood. Job had challenged the manner of God's control; hence God's response challenges Job in turn. Just what does this Creator God intend to teach? Is the display of cosmic wonders meant to dazzle Job with the magnitude of God's creative ability? Is the train of rare animals paraded before Job aimed at confounding him with their grace and agility or their awesome dimensions? Is God merely concerned with forcing a confession of weakness and pride from this man who is already reduced to almost nothing? Will this show of unquestioned divine superiority be enough to quell Job's turmoil, end his pleading, and satisfy his demand for an explanation?

God's speeches are considered some of the most beautiful nature poetry of the Ancient Near East. God quizzes Job about the marvels of divine creative power and its extraordinary management of the universe. His ability to exercise control over wild beasts or fathom some of the unique characteristics of the animal realm is contested. Job can only stand in awe of the magnificent governing structure within the universe that far exceeds human comprehension or control (40:4–5). The descriptions of Behemoth and Leviathan (40:15—41:26) suggest that they are two great mythological creatures of chaos. It is clear that these fearsome beasts are no threat to God. In fact, Behemoth is identified as a creature of God (40:19), and Leviathan is depicted as a domesticated pet (41:1–11). If God can bridle the monsters of chaos, then divine control is indeed exercised in each and every realm of creation, whether mythological, material, or moral.

Job demanded insight into the circumstances of his life. In response, God redirects Job's attention to the broader universe and asks questions about comprehension and control. Using nature in an analogical fashion, God brings Job to a new horizon of understanding and trust. If he cannot imagine the ways that God continues to sustain creation, how can he possibly fathom God's mysterious care in his own life? Job now realizes that his own limited human ability to comprehend must not be the measure of God's providence.

The last words that Job utters are found in his reply to God's second speech:

> "I have uttered what I did not understand,
> things too wonderful for me,
>   which I did not know." (Job 42:3)

> "I . . . repent in dust and ashes." (Job 42:6)

These words show that the opposing tensions with which Job had struggled have been reconciled. Yet how can this be, if his questions about justice have not been answered? Of what does he repent if he is an innocent sufferer? In his anguish Job had claimed that his predicament was proof that God did not have the power to ensure that innocence would be protected and wickedness redressed. The speeches demonstrated that God is indeed in control. In fact, this control far exceeds anything Job could have imagined.

Job repents, but not because he lacked integrity; he repents because he lacked vision. This lack of vision became obvious when he was unable to answer the questions about nature put to him by God. As teacher, not judge, God led Job to see that just as there are mysteries in nature beyond human understanding and control, so there are mysteries in the way life unfolds that mere human beings will never be able to grasp. Job admits that only God is unlimited in wisdom and power. He, Job, is human and finite. God has complete control over all of creation and cares for it with providence beyond human comprehension. This is all that Job needs to know. He can trust such a God and live with his unanswered questions. Although Job never intended to usurp any divine privilege or status, his anthropological presuppositions were exaggerated. The divine speeches corrected these presuppositions by pointing out time and again that God is God, and Job is not.

The splendor of creation transcends Job's comprehension, and he can only stand in awe and wonder. His former questions may not have been answered in the way they had been asked, nor were his demands met, but his fears were dissipated and his trust in God restored. Job's struggle, which began with unexplained suffering and moved to an unfulfilled expectation of comprehension, was taken out of the narrow realm of anthropology and placed within the expansive context of cosmology. His legitimate human concerns were never minimized by God. However, a manifestation of the divine power that brought forth and continues to provide for all creation brought Job to realize that, though he was not in control of the community of Earth, he was a vital member of it, and God was in control.

Several ecojustice principles are operative in this story. Job's inability to understand or control aspects of the cosmos and various animals of Earth are evidence that their value is intrinsic to them and not determined by their usefulness to human beings. The principle of purpose is also evident. It states that "the universe, Earth and all its components are part of a dynamic cosmic design within which each piece has a place in the overall goal of that design."[7] Job's ultimate struggle was not merely with the suffering that he endured, but with his inability to understand why he had to endure it. He presumed that he should be able to grasp the unfolding of human life and understand the way it functioned. God's questioning brought him to see that human

---

[7] Ibid.

life is part of the design of the entire cosmos, and understanding the cosmos is far beyond human comprehension.

The Figure of Wisdom

The mysterious figure of a woman moves through several major books that make up the Wisdom tradition—Proverbs 8—9, Wisdom of Solomon 7—9, Sirach 24, and Baruch 4. It is the figure of Wisdom personified. Personification, the literary technique in which a human feature is attributed to a nonhuman being, is a common feature of poetry. In the Bible it is frequently found in prophetic writing:

> Break out together in song, O ruins of Jerusa-
> lem. (Isa 52:9)

as well as in the psalms:

> Let the rivers clap their hands,
>   and the mountains shout with them for joy.
>   (Ps 98:7)

However, in cases such as these, the characterization is simply a poetic device, a kind of metaphoric expression. The characterization of Woman Wisdom is entirely different. Several explanations for such a personification have been suggested. Some commentators believe that the figure of Woman Wisdom can be traced back to an Ancient Near Eastern goddess of wisdom, one that the Israelites might have known or even worshiped. The Phoenicians' goddess Ishtar has been suggested, as has the Egyptian goddess Ma'at. Those who hold this view claim that over time what Israel once revered as a goddess with her own unique identity was eventually considered a characteristic of the sole true God. This view corresponds to what scholars have long believed about Israel moving from believing in many gods (polytheism), to maintaining that among all the gods venerated in the ancient world, Israel was to worship only one god (monolatry), to insisting that there is only one God, and that is the God who chose to enter into covenant with Israel (monotheism).

Other interpreters argue that Israel never revered Wisdom as a deity, but always considered it a personified characteristic of God. Such a characterization is known as hypostasis, a technique in which a personal trait is perceived as an individual with its own existence. The biblical passages that describe Wisdom's origin clearly state that she was created and that she had a life of her own. They also describe her as a creature with cosmic dimensions, existing before the rest of creation was called into being and active beyond the confines of space and time. These features suggest a mythological origin. Such an interpretation would not be foreign to Israelite thinking, for there are several other places in the Bible that contain mythological elements, passages such as the garden with the talking serpent (Gen 2—3) and the battle with the sea dragon (Isa 27:1).

Still other interpreters consider the personification as a creative literary device. Some of these interpreters regard it as merely an artistic development stemming from the Hebrew word for wisdom *(hokmah)*, which is the feminine form of a verbal root. Another literary explanation is far more highly developed. It regards the personification as a religious symbol prominent during the postexilic period that acted as a mediator describing the relationship between God and the people.

Whatever the origin of this enigmatic figure, Woman Wisdom probably represents that inaccessible dimension of wisdom that we all desire but which resides with God alone; the kind of wisdom that is within creation but beyond us; wisdom that explains the universe but which we cannot attain. This mysterious figure, whatever her origin, reminds us that the fullness of wisdom cannot be gained through limited human experience. It belongs to God.

The connection between Woman Wisdom and creation is clearly seen in two major passages (Prov 8:22–31 and Sir 24:1–6). The passage from Proverbs is perhaps the best known:

> The LORD created me at the beginning of his
>   work,
>   the first of his acts of long ago.
> Ages ago I was set up,
>   at the first, before the beginning of the
>   earth.

When there were no depths I was brought forth,
   when there were no springs abounding
     with water.
Before the mountains had been shaped,
   before the hills, I was brought forth—
when he had not yet made earth and fields,
   or the world's first bits of soil.
When he established the heavens, I was there,
   when he drew a circle on the face of the
     deep,
when he made firm the skies above,
   when he established the fountains of the
     deep,
when he assigned to the sea its limit,
   so that the waters might not transgress his
     command,
when he marked out the foundations of the
     earth,
   then I was beside him, like a master
     worker;
and I was daily his delight,
   rejoicing before him always,
rejoicing in his inhabited world
   and delighting in the human race. (Prov
     8:22–31)

In this self-proclamation Woman Wisdom clearly states that she is not divine; she was created by God. She was, however, the first to come forth from God. The creation of the natural world that she preceded is vast in scope. It stretches from the watery depths to the highest mountains; it includes both Earth and the heavens. Even the forces of chaos (the deep) have been restrained by God's creative power. Woman Wisdom here identifies herself as a "master worker" and architect, suggesting that she played some role in this vast creation. Perhaps it is the order in creation that can be observed that has led some to argue that Wisdom is not only closely associated with creation, but that creation actually conforms to a design that originated with her.

The idea of Woman Wisdom as the architect of creation calls to mind the concept of the Urmensch or Primordial Man that was derived from Iranian myths and was widespread in the Ancient Near East. This individual, not to be confused with the first created man, was really a cosmological being, the macrocosm from which creation, the microcosm, was formed. There are significant differences here, however. The Primordial Man was more or less divine; Woman Wisdom is not. In the Iranian myth the cosmos actually came from the Primordial Man; Woman Wisdom is not the creator but merely played a role in the drama of creation.

Finally, Woman Wisdom emphatically states that she takes delight in God's creation. This is a very important point and will be developed later.

A second passage that links Woman Wisdom with creation is found in Sirach:

> "I came forth from the mouth of the Most
> High,
> and covered the earth like a mist.
> I dwelt in the highest heavens,
> and my throne was in a pillar of cloud.
> Alone I compassed the vault of heaven
> and traversed the depths of the abyss.
> Over waves of the sea, over all the earth,
> and over every people and nation I have
> held sway." (Sir 24:3–6)

Certain aspects of this description of Woman Wisdom border on the divine. Like God, she is enthroned above the clouds and holds sway over creation, from the depths of the sea to the heights of heaven. These are divine characteristics. However, at the outset she acknowledges that she is not divine, but that she came forth from God. Thus, the honor that she enjoys and the dominion that she exercises over all creation are not hers by right but have been delegated to her by the Creator God.

The figure of Woman Wisdom is compatible with important ecojustice principles. First and most important, it is clear that in this tradition the community of Earth is cherished because of its intrinsic value. Creation comes from God, and it is entrusted to Woman Wisdom to oversee so that it can be true to its unique nature and goal, not so that it can meet the goals of human beings.

Second, Woman Wisdom, the overseer and perhaps designer of Earth, takes delight in God's creation. She appreciates the community of Earth as a whole and each member of it individually. Though these texts do not explicitly speak of interconnectedness and interdependence, mention of specific members of this community—mountains, hills, fields, and soil (Proverbs); every people and nation (Sirach)—suggests respect for diversity within the whole community. Finally, if Woman Wisdom acted as a master worker or architect, then she is responsible for the "dynamic cosmic design within which each piece has a place in the overall goal of that design."[8]

Praise the LORD!

The psalms have been known, loved, and prayed by religious people from the time of their origin to our own day. Even those who have little or no biblical knowledge recognize themes and phrases from the psalms. They have been woven into the very fabric of the great literature of Western civilization and have been the inspiration for some of its most beautiful music. The psalms continue to be the backbone of both liturgical prayer and personal devotion.

There are several different types of psalms, but all of them express some kind of religious sentiment. One of the best-known types is the hymn. This is a song in praise of God's goodness and majesty. It acclaims both the creative and the redemptive acts of God. One of the most widely known hymns is Psalm 8:

> O LORD, our Sovereign,
>   how majestic is your name in all the earth!
> You have set your glory above the heavens.
>   Out of the mouths of babes and infants
> you have founded a bulwark
>   because of your foes, to silence the enemy
>   and the avenger.
> When I look at your heavens, the work of your
>   fingers,

---

[8] Ibid.

the moon and the stars that you have
    established;
what are human beings that you are mindful
    of them,
    mortals that you care for them?
Yet you have made them a little lower than
    God,
    and crowned them with glory and honor.
You have given them dominion over the works
    of your hands;
    you have put all things under their feet,
all sheep and oxen,
    and also the beasts of the field,
the birds of the air, and the fish of the sea,
    whatever passes along the paths of the seas.
O LORD, our Sovereign,
    how majestic is your name in all the earth!
    (Ps 8:1–9)

In this psalm the reason for praising God is the wondrous creation that God has brought forth. Attention is drawn first to
the principal heavenly bodies, whose splendor and greatness
prompted many cultures to consider them deities. This resplen-
dence is next compared with the relative insignificance of human beings. Two Hebrew words characterize the lowly nature
of humankind: *enosh*, which means "weak human being"; and
ben-adam, which is translated "son of the one formed from the
ground." Just as early in the psalm the most vulnerable (babes
and infants) were contrasted with the powerful (foes, enemy,
avenger), so limited humankind is compared with the glorious
heavenly bodies. Though inferior to heavenly wonders, human
beings are still exalted creatures. Royal imagery describing
their lofty status—"crowned them with glory and honor"—is
complemented by a reference to the responsibility they bear for
the rest of the created world—"given them dominion over the
works of your hands."

These verses call to mind the description of the role played
by human beings found in the first account of creation, that is,
"subdue . . . and have dominion" (Gen 1:28). This single verse

has been cited by many as biblical justification for human domination over the rest of the created world and for exploitation of the riches of creation for human goals.[9] However, interpreting both the Genesis account and Psalm 8 in this way actually misunderstands the commission found in both passages.

In the first creation account the man and the woman are said to have been made in the image of God (Gen 1:26). While "image of God" has been interpreted in many ways down through the centuries, its original meaning probably had something to do with the monarchy. People in the Ancient Near East often set up images of their monarchs, whom they thought were divine. Such an image was regarded as a marker that identified the place and the scope of the sovereignty of the ruler. (Today, a national flag functions in a comparable manner.) The image was merely a representation of the god; it possessed no authority of its own. Israelite law banned the practice of fashioning such images, for too often the people failed to distinguish between the image and the god it represented. In such cases the reverence given the image degenerated into worship of it, as if the image were actually the god.

The man and the woman in the Genesis account were not divine. Rather, as "image of God" they represented the sovereignty of God. The twofold injunction found in this account reinforces the royal motif. They are told to subdue (any threat that might arise) and have dominion (as overseers of the realm or agents of God). These were clearly responsibilities that belonged to monarchy. Because of the longstanding misinterpretation of this tradition, one cannot emphasize enough the fact that the Israelite monarchy was not autonomous in its governance. Since an image represented the place and scope of the sovereignty of God and not any privilege of the image itself, it is clear that the monarchy's authority was provisional and contingent on the good will of God. Israelite royalty was accountable to God for overseeing and nurturing the members of the community of Earth. Without denying the unique standing human beings enjoy

---

[9] For a stern criticism of this understanding of the biblical passage along with the exploitation that it engendered, see Lynn White, "The Religious Roots of Our Ecological Crisis," *Science* 155 (1967): 1203–7.

within this community, they are still creatures, responsible for the well-being of creation and accountable to God for the way they manage it.

With this understanding, it is clear that while Psalm 8 underscores the unique place of human beings within the natural world, it is a place of both responsibility and accountability, not of unbridled self-gratification and exploitation. Furthermore, the psalm is praising God for the glories of creation, not the creatures themselves. This is clear from the refrain with which the psalm both opens and closes:

> O LORD, our Sovereign,
> how majestic is your name in all the earth!
> (Ps 8:1, 10)

A second psalm that focuses on the creator who has brought the world into existence rather than on the components of creation is Psalm 104, which is considered by many to be the most beautiful psalm of the entire Psalter. Though it is a long psalm, its creative composition and the comprehensiveness of its reflection on natural creation are best seen when the entire psalm is read. Commentators divide the strophes in various ways. The following divisions have been determined by content and represent a general consensus among the scholars.

vv. 1–4 Call to praise God who fashioned a heavenly throne room:

> Bless the LORD, O my soul.
> O LORD my God, you are very great.
> You are clothed with honor and majesty,
> wrapped in light as with a garment.
> You stretch out the heavens like a tent,
> you set the beams of your chambers on the
> waters,
> you make the clouds your chariot,
> you ride on the wings of the wind,
> you make the winds your messengers,
> fire and flame your ministers.

vv. 5–9 God conquered chaotic primeval waters and founded Earth:

> You set the earth on its foundations,
>> so that it shall never be shaken.
> You cover it with the deep as with a garment;
>> the waters stood above the mountains.
> At your rebuke they flee;
>> at the sound of your thunder they take to
>> flight.
> They rose up to the mountains,
>> ran down to the valleys to the place that
>> you appointed for them.
> You set a boundary that they may not pass,
>> so that they might not again cover the
>> earth.

vv. 10–18 God provides for the community of Earth:

> You make springs gush forth in the valleys;
>> they flow between the hills,
> giving drink to every wild animal;
>> the wild asses quench their thirst.
> By the streams the birds of the air have their
>> habitation;
>> they sing among the branches.
> From your lofty abode you water the moun-
>> tains;
>> the earth is satisfied with the fruit of your
>> work.
> You cause the grass to grow for the cattle,
>> and plants for people to use,
> to bring forth food from the earth,
>> and wine to gladden the human heart,
> oil to make the face shine,
>> and bread to strengthen the human heart.
> The trees of the LORD are watered abundantly,
>> the cedars of Lebanon that he planted.
> In them the birds build their nests;
>> the stork has its home in the fir trees.

> The high mountains are for the wild goats;
> the rocks are a refuge for the coneys.

vv. 19–24 God governs night and day

> You have made the moon to mark the sea-
> sons;
> the sun knows its time for setting.
> You make darkness, and it is night,
> when all the animals of the forest come
> creeping out.
> The young lions roar for their prey,
> seeking their food from God.
> When the sun rises, they withdraw
> and lie down in their dens.
> People go out to their work
> and to their labor until the evening.

vv. 25–26 God governs the powers of the sea

> O Lord, how manifold are your works!
> In wisdom you have made them all;
> the earth is full of your creatures.
> Yonder is the sea, great and wide,
> creeping things innumerable are there,
> living things both small and great.
> There go the ships,
> and Leviathan that you formed to sport in
> it.

vv. 27–30 Life and death are in God's hands

> These all look to you
> to give them their food in due season;
> when you give to them, they gather it up;
> when you open your hand, they are filled
> with good things.
> When you hide your face, they are dismayed;
> when you take away their breath, they die
> and return to their dust.

> When you send forth your spirit, they are cre-
> ated;
> and you renew the face of the ground.

vv. 31–35 Hymnic ending

> May the glory of the LORD endure forever;
>   may the LORD rejoice in his works—
> who looks on the earth and it trembles,
>   who touches the mountains and they
>   smoke.
> I will sing to the LORD as long as I live;
>   I will sing praise to my God while I have
>   being.
> May my meditation be pleasing to him,
>   for I rejoice in the LORD.
> Let sinners be consumed from the earth,
>   and let the wicked be no more.
> Bless the LORD, O my soul.
> Praise the LORD! (Ps 104:1–35)

Although most of this psalm bears a close resemblance to the Egyptian "Hymn to the Sun" ascribed to the great pharaoh Akhenaton (ca. 1364–1347 BCE), reference to primeval waters was probably Canaanite in origin. Despite these influences, Israelite monotheism holds sway throughout the psalm. It is God who created, supports, and governs the entire community of Earth. Human beings belong to this world, but only as creatures dependent on the Creator God like every other creature. In fact, they constitute a very small fraction of the creatures of Earth. They are simply coinhabitants like the storks and the coneys. They are not depicted as overseers, as in Psalm 8, and they are certainly not rulers, as Psalm 8 is often misinterpreted to mean. Psalm 104 ends with a prayer that God will continue to sustain the marvels of creation, and that sinners will have no power to threaten them.

No doubt the Psalmist had the possibility of divine punishment in mind when writing: "Let sinners be consumed from the earth, and let the wicked be no more." Contemporary readers who are aware of the devastating effects of the human exploitation of elements of the natural world might understand this verse in a slightly different way. Rather than a plea that God step in and directly punish sinners, they might see it as a prayer for a change of heart of those guilty of exploitation.

Finally, Psalm 104 revels in the magnificence and diversity of the components that make up our cosmos. This psalm acclaims not only *creatio prima*, the initial act of creation, but also *creatio continuata*, the ongoing flourishing of life. Creation is seen as good, without any defect. In the face of such panoply of wonder, an appropriate response can only be to "Praise the Lord!"

Various hymns include an acclamation or a refrain, the most recurring one being "Praise the Lord!" A group known as the Hallel psalms (Psalms 146—150), from the Hebrew *Hallelujah* or "Praise the Lord," acclaim God as the creator of the universe. One psalm in this group is particularly relevant to this discussion, for it calls on natural creation itself to praise God:

> Praise the LORD!
> Praise the LORD from the heavens;
>   praise him in the heights!
> Praise him, all his angels;
>   praise him, all his host!
> Praise him, sun and moon;
>   praise him, all you shining stars!
> Praise him, you highest heavens,
>   and you waters above the heavens!
> Let them praise the name of the LORD,
>   for he commanded and they were created.
> He established them forever and ever;
>   he fixed their bounds, which cannot be
>   passed.
> Praise the LORD from the earth,
>   you sea monsters and all deeps,
> fire and hail, snow and frost,
>   stormy wind fulfilling his command!
> Mountains and all hills,
>   fruit trees and all cedars!

> Wild animals and all cattle,
>   creeping things and flying birds!
> Kings of the earth and all peoples,
>   princes and all rulers of the earth!
> Young men and women alike,
>   old and young together!
> Let them praise the name of the LORD,
>   for his name alone is exalted;
>   his glory is above earth and heaven.
> He has raised up a horn for his people,
>   praise for all his faithful,
>   for the people of Israel who are close to him.
> Praise the LORD! (Ps 148:1–14)

The layout of this psalm is the same as that found in other biblical creation texts, such as the speeches of God (Job 38), the "Song of the Young Men" in the fiery furnace (Dan 3:54–83),[10] the praise of creation (Sirach 43). This cosmological inventory resembles the order found in the ancient Egyptian Teaching of Amenemope (ca. 1300–1075 BCE): heaven, sun, moon, stars, sea of heaven, primeval waters, lightning, hail, snow, storms, mountain, hill, trees, animals, and groups of people. These similarities notwithstanding, Psalm 148 is unique in that it does not merely rejoice in the marvels of the created world, but it actually calls all creatures to praise God.

The first part of the psalm calls on the forces of heaven to praise God, forces that in the ancient world were often thought to be deities themselves. In the second part components of Earth are summoned. None of the components of Earth is seen as evil, neither the chaotic monsters of the deep nor the predatory animals of the wild. In other words their natures are not judged by human standards but by the fact that they have been created by God. One might ask: How do inanimate creatures praise God? In answer: They praise God by being true to their natures. This is clear in both verse 5b:

> Let them praise the name of the LORD,
>   for his name alone is exalted;

---

[10] Greek version.

and verse 6:

> He established them forever and ever;
>   he fixed their bounds, which cannot be
>   passed.

The creatures, all of them, were created by God and given a specific place in the created order.

In praising God, Earth creatures have voice, one of the eco-justice principles by which biblical passages are analyzed in this book. Here, voice is a metaphor that refers to a manner of communication. The metaphor itself might be anthropocentric, but the metaphor's function is theocentric, not anthropocentric; the community of Earth is called to praise God, not to praise human beings.

These psalms of praise all appreciate members of the community of Earth for their intrinsic value as creatures of God. Psalm 8, in the spirit of Genesis 1, understands human uniqueness as a responsibility with corresponding accountability. Psalm 104 manifests the interconnectedness of all creation. Psalm 148 is distinctive in that it depicts creatures of Earth as possessing voice and using it to praise God.

The Way of Wisdom

While it is true that Wisdom focuses on the design of the natural world in order to lead human beings to successful living, it does not subordinate that world to human desires. Just the opposite. As the Greeks understood catholicity, human beings are meant to live in harmony with the forces of the natural world. Attuned to this understanding, the basis of the pedagogical approach employed by the sages of ancient Israel was grounded in the realization of the integrity of the natural world itself. The sages did not attempt to accommodate that world to human plans, but rather to direct human beings to accommodate themselves to nature's design. This can be seen in the nature proverbs used to exhort appropriate behavior, in the way aspects of creation brought Job to acknowledge God's providential care, in the manner in which nature led Qoheleth to live in the present moment, in Woman

Wisdom's management of creation, and in the way the creatures give praise to God by being faithful to their respective natures.

The Wisdom tradition is perhaps the Bible's prime example of a mindset that recognized the fact of intrinsic catholicity, of all things attuned to the physical order, of living in harmony with the cosmos. Though attentive to human concerns, it sought to bring those concerns into harmony with the natural world. Accordingly, passages from this tradition can be retrieved and recontextualized in a contemporary setting without revision.

The way of wisdom today leads us into a new cosmological consciousness borne of the realization that our universe is evolving into something new rather than remaining static. Insights such as those discussed in this chapter are not lost in this new realization. Rather, they are enhanced. Recognizing the interconnectedness and interdependence of members of the community of Earth, we are challenged to reform the way we live within that community. With Job we can see our suffering as part of the groaning of creation eager to be transformed into something greater. Accepting the ambiguities of life, like Qoheleth, can encourage us to live in trust in the present moment, open to the emerging possibilities of the future. Acknowledging that the management of the world is really not in our hands, as Woman Wisdom's sway reveals, can instill in us an appreciation of divine providence over the entire created world. Learning from the natural world in these ways, we will finally come to see that there is indeed a dynamic, evolving design to the entire universe and that the greatest praise we can offer God is being faithful to the unique role we play as human beings in that design.

"Who do you say that I am?"

—Matthew 16:13; Mark 8:29; Luke 9:20

Chapter Five

We now move from the traditions of ancient Israel to those of early Christianity. Since Jesus and most of his earliest followers were steeped in the traditions of their Israelite ancestors, we should not be surprised that they shared a cosmological worldview similar to those ancestors. This worldview is the stage on which the drama found in the Gospels unfolds.

For many people, a gospel is a history of Jesus of Nazareth, recounting events of his life and death and containing stories of his disciples' encounters with him after his resurrection. However, a gospel is a much richer and more complex kind of story. The word itself means "good news," and this good news originated as an oral proclamation or announcement. The question is: Proclamation or announcement of what?

After Jesus's resurrection, stories about him were told by his followers. This form of remembering him usually took place when the community of believers gathered for prayer. Stories were also told when those believers went out to others, proclaiming Jesus as the one sent by God to the world. In such remembering and proclaiming, the stories were often fashioned to the needs of the audience. This partly explains why there are various versions of the same story. The very earliest stories were probably testimonies of encounters with the risen Jesus. Reports of events that took place during his public ministry were then added to these accounts, as were explanations of the message that he preached. Once these various accounts were collected, stories about his birth were often added. This process of literary formation took several years and produced numerous gospels, only four of which were considered canonical—Matthew, Mark, Luke, and John.[1] Each narrates its stories through its own particular theological lenses and does so with specific literary and theological emphases. The passages examined in this chapter take account of some of these differences.

Literary Context

In order to grasp the profound meaning of the message of the gospel we must understand the kind of literature used to proclaim this message. The discrepancies among the various stories suggest that historical accuracy was not a major goal for those telling the story or those hearing it. For example, in the Synoptic Gospels (Matthew, Mark, and Luke), the adult Jesus only goes to Jerusalem once, at which time he is captured and put to death. In John's Gospel, he goes several times to celebrate major feasts. Other inconsistencies are found in both the birth accounts in Matthew and Luke and in details of Jesus's passion and crucifixion. How are these discrepancies to be understood? Are the Gospels in error? A look at the literary form of the gospel will help to answer such questions.

Most scholars maintain that the gospel is a unique kind of literature. While it has characteristics of at least two ancient forms, the laudatory biography and the encomium, it really stands by itself as a literary form. A laudatory biography follows a particular pattern. It begins with narratives that describe events surrounding the birth of the individual, followed by episodes from that person's life, ending with a death account. Matthew and Luke certainly follow this pattern, while Mark and John lack birth narratives. What is notable about the Gospels is not their conformity to the pattern of this kind of biography, but

---

[1] Other gospels considered apocryphal and not included in the Bible are the Gospel of Thomas, the Gospel of Peter, the Gospel of Nicodemus, the Gospel of the Nazoreans, the Gospel of the Ebionites, the Gospel of the Hebrews, the Gospel of the Egyptians, the Gospel of Philip, and the Gospel of Mary.

the character of the stories themselves. Unlike the historical biography, which is concerned with precise details, the laudatory biography exaggerates details in order to underscore the importance or majesty of the person being praised. In the ancient world, such exaggeration often took the form of mythological metaphor. For example, a person who would make a significant difference in the world was often depicted as possessing more than human qualities, sometimes conversing with the gods and being preserved from the limitations that burden ordinary human beings. Such a description might not have been historically accurate, but it captured the significance of the individual for those revering that person more than precise details could. This is the primary difference between the historical biography, so important to us today, and the laudatory biography so common in the ancient world.

An encomium is similar to but shorter than a laudatory biography. Its purpose is to heap praise on an individual. When military leaders returned home after a victory, an encomium was frequently offered in praise of their valor and military accomplishments. Encomiums also served as eulogies. While this form of praise reviews the life of the individual, it also contains a prologue and an epilogue, features not found in the laudatory biography. The first fifteen verses of John's Gospel, in which Jesus is identified as the Word of God through whom the universe was created, are often considered a prologue, similar to that found in an encomium.

To say that the Gospels are not literal biographies of Jesus does not suggest that they have no historical value at all. The issue of historical value has been a concern of the church for decades, particularly since methods of contemporary critical interpretation have thrown the historical character of the Gospels into question.[2] In 1964, the Pontifical Biblical Commission issued a document entitled "Instruction on the Historical Truth of the Gospels." In it, the commission described three stages of gospel formation. The first stage addresses issues pertaining to the actual

---

[2] At one end of this issue are those who hold that everything in the Gospels should be understood literally. At the other end are interpreters, like those in the Jesus Seminar, who reject the historicity of most of what the Gospels state.

public ministry of Jesus. It consists of memories of what he did and said. It is important to remember that in an oral culture, people's memories are much more accurate than are those of people in a literate culture, for the history of the people is preserved in those memories rather than in written form. The second stage of gospel formation is that of the apostolic teaching of the immediate followers of Jesus. The collective memories of this group were adapted to the needs and concerns of new audiences. The Jewish or Gentile character of this audience influenced the character of the adaptation. Finally, these adapted memories were written down. This is the stage of the gospel writer. Throughout this process the historical authority of the memories lies less in their specific details than in fidelity to their fundamental religious meaning. It is in this same spirit of fidelity that contemporary commentators interpret the message of the Gospels for today.

The four canonical Gospels seek to portray Jesus in more than human form. Some gospel stories depict him as the long-awaited messiah; in others he is identified as the mysterious Son of man; in still others his divine powers are evident. Since these aspects of his identity are spiritual, they were not always obvious. Thus they are presented by the gospel writers in extraordinary ways so that they can be recognized.

One can conclude, therefore, that the Gospels are not in error. Rather, they are more than historical eyewitness accounts. They are a unique literary form that praises Jesus for who he is and for what he did. Apparent discrepancies are simply various points of view resulting from the desire of the writers to emphasize different aspects of Jesus to distinctive audiences.

"King of the Jews"

Though most scholars today believe that Mark is the oldest Gospel, Matthew appears first in canonical order. The similarities it bears to Mark are considered literary evidence of its dependence on that earlier Gospel. Though it follows the order of Mark, Matthew contains sayings of Jesus not found there as well as many original narratives. Even the stories that are similar often provide a slightly different point of view because of the literary context within which they are found and the variations in language.

The Jewish roots of Matthew's Gospel have long been recognized. The Gospel opens with a genealogy that first identifies Jesus as the messiah, the son of David, and then places him squarely within the history of Israel. The very structure of the genealogy reinforces Jesus's Davidic lineage. This list of ancestors is divided into three sections, each containing fourteen names, fourteen being the numerical value of the name David. This is something Jews would recognize. Israelite connections are also seen in the frequent use of Old Testament passages to throw light on the meaning of Jesus's words and actions. Finally, this Gospel shows obvious concern for Jewish Law and customs. The fact that the implications of the Law and the meaning of the customs are presumed rather than explained implies a Jewish audience of this Gospel. All of this suggests that one of the goals of this Gospel is to show that Jesus is indeed the fulfillment of the promises made to the ancestors of the Jewish people and to bring to fruition their religious expectations.

Many of the sayings found in Matthew's Gospel provide glimpses into the cosmological worldview that seems to have remained basically the same throughout all three stages of gospel formation. However, since this study does not presume to address all possible issues, only two passages are examined: the account of the star over Bethlehem (Matt 2:2–10), and the description of cosmological disturbance at the time of Jesus's death (Matt 27:45–52).

The appearance of the star is found in the account of the visit of the magi:

> In the time of King Herod, after Jesus was born in Bethlehem of Judea, wise men from the East came to Jerusalem, asking, "Where is the child who has been born king of the Jews? For we observed his star at its rising, and have come to pay him homage." . . . Then Herod secretly called for the wise men and learned from them the exact time when the star had appeared. . . . When they had heard the king, they set out; and there, ahead of them, went the star that they had seen at its rising, until it stopped over the place where

the child was. When they saw that the star had stopped, they were overwhelmed with joy. (Matt 2:1–2, 7, 9–10)

The idea that the birth of an important person was heralded by a celestial event was a common theme in the ancient world. The Roman poet Virgil wrote that a star guided Aeneas to the place where Rome was later founded; Persian astrologers claimed that a remarkable light foreshadowed the birth of Alexander the Great; the same was said about Caesar Augustus. Were these actual celestial events, or was this a literary explanation meant to underscore the importance of these people? The same question might be asked about the star of Bethlehem. Astrological records suggest that such an event did indeed take place sometime during the years that surround Jesus's birth. But, what was it? And what did it mean?

Three astronomical events have been advanced as explanation of the nature of this star.[3] All of them are natural phenomena. Some commentators suggest that it was a supernova or new star, one that can seem brighter than other celestial bodies and even be seen during the day. This explanation corresponds to the description found in the Gospel. However, there is no record that such an event occurred around the date usually said to be the year Jesus was born (ca. 6 BCE). A second possibility is a comet. Two confirmed historical events strengthen this possibility: the appearance of Halley's comet in 12 BCE and the arrival of foreign diplomats two years later to celebrate the completion of the city and harbor of Caesarea Maritima on the Mediterranean coast of Israel built by King Herod. But while comets are remarkably bright and usually flash across the sky with a luminous tail, in the ancient world they were considered harbingers of bad news. Therefore, the Bethlehem star was probably not a comet.

Today, most commentators believe that what was seen as an unusual star was probably caused by the conjunction of the planets Jupiter and Saturn, which occurs every twenty years. On rare occasions Mars passes close to this conjunction, thus adding to the brilliance of the event. The renowned seventeenth-century

---

[3] Much of the information about the star is found in Raymond E. Brown, SS, "The Birth of the Messiah," 170–74, in *The Anchor Bible Reference Library* (New York: Doubleday, 1992).

German mathematician and astronomer Johannes Kepler calculated that this threefold conjunction occurs every 805 years, and that it happened in 7–6 BCE. This historical evidence suggests that, whether the details as found in the Matthean passage are accurate or not, such a celestial appearance did occur around the time of the birth of Jesus. This raises an important question: Was his birth the cause of the celestial event, or did the event provide believers a symbol for understanding Jesus in a particular way?

Early Christians with Jewish roots did not have to look outside of their religious heritage to find a tradition about a wise man and a star. In one of the visions of the non-Israelite prophet Balaam, a star is linked to a future king:

> A star shall come out of Jacob,
>   and a scepter shall rise out of Israel. (Num
>   24:17)

Most interpreters hold that this is a reference to the Davidic monarchy, a tradition that Christians believe finds its fulfillment in Jesus. Still the question about origin must be asked: Was the light in the sky occasioned by the birth of Jesus, or was an already present heavenly light interpreted as a traditional sign of the birth of a great person? Believers at each stage of the formation of the Gospel probably understood the celestial marvel as related exclusively with the birth of Jesus. Contemporary believers probably hold a different point of view. Since their cosmology is less mythological and more scientific, they are likely to argue that such events need not be caused by extraordinary divine intervention. Rather, such events are the result of heavenly bodies following their own natural laws. In other words, this already present celestial marvel was later associated with the birth of Jesus.

The difference between these two views is significant. The ecojustice principle of value highlights that difference. In the first view the existence and meaning of the phenomenon are dependent upon and merely reflective of the importance of the revered person. From this point of view the celestial event itself has only instrumental value. On the other hand, the intrinsic value of the occurrence is in the forefront in the second view. There the celestial event is seen as the result of the conjunction of heavenly bodies, independent of any birth. In this view the inherent integrity of the natural event influences the way its association with the person is interpreted. The marvel of the event is here appropriated to the importance of the person without the event losing any of its intrinsic value.

Such demythologizing of what was thought to be miraculous does not diminish the extraordinary and unparalleled reality of Jesus. The fact that he is so described indicates that his followers recognized him as extraordinary, but with eyes of faith rather than through some physical manifestation. His followers believe that an indescribable light came into the world with his birth. How better to acknowledge this than to clothe this celestial event with standard metaphoric garb that marks his distinction?

Just as the birth of Jesus is linked to a splendid celestial occurrence, so the details of his death include extraordinary terrestrial occurrences:

> From noon on, darkness came over the whole land until three in the afternoon. . . . At that moment the curtain of the temple was torn in two, from top to bottom. The earth shook, and the rocks were split. The tombs also were opened, and many bodies of the saints who had fallen asleep were raised. (Matt 27:45, 51–52)

Once again we are faced with several questions. The first is one of historicity: Were these real occurrences, or were they literary devices developed out of standard themes associated with the death of a great person?[4] Darkness in the middle of the day was not impossible. A solar eclipse could have caused it; or, since the Temple was open to the east, a sirocco wind off the desert could have brought about a dust or sand storm causing both darkness and damage to the temple veil; or, residue from volcanic activity in the mountains could also have obscured the light of the sun; or, a thunderstorm might be the cause. Eclipses in the vicinity and during the correct time period have been recorded. Ancient writers such as Origen, Eusebius, Cicero,

---

[4] See Raymond E. Brown, SS, "The Death of the Messiah," 2:1041–43, in *The Anchor Bible Reference Library* (New York: Doubleday, 1994).

and Josephus all mention such remarkable signs. Though authors have been known to exaggerate the duration of an eclipse in order to emphasize the importance of some person, an eclipse lasts ten minutes at the most, not three hours as the Gospel indicates. Such records notwithstanding, a solar eclipse would not occur during the period of full moon, which is when Passover is celebrated. Most likely, there was no eclipse. Darkness from storms is always a possibility, but there is no ancient record that authenticates one as Matthew describes it. Most commentators think these natural events are unlikely. If this is correct, why does the gospel writer include them, and what do they mean?

Ominous darkness and menacing upheavals of Earth such as earthquake, the opening of tombs, and the raising of the dead are apocalyptic signs of the great suffering known in Jewish tradition as the "birthpangs of the messiah" (see Matt 24:8; Mark 13:8; Rom 8:22). This expression refers to the suffering that people believed would precede the inauguration of the messianic age or time of fulfillment. It seems that the gospel writer included these occurrences in the description of the death of Jesus so that the reader would realize that his death ushered in this new age. If these natural features are really a traditional way of recounting the death of an exceptional person, one might conclude that their value is simply instrumental, a way of describing the significance of the death of a human being. However, one can interpret these remarkable events in another way, a way that underscores their intrinsic value.

Darkness, earthquakes, and the splitting of rocks result from components of Earth following their natural laws as they adjust to physical changes within their respective ecosystems. Human beings interpret these events from their limited anthropocentric point of view and devise literary explanations that reflect this point of view. This explanation then enhances the way we understand death. In this case the importance of Jesus, rather than the laws of nature that components of Earth follow, is thought to cause the extraordinary occurrence. Thus it is precisely the power in the volatile events that provides an understanding of the "birthpangs of the messiah."

As with the interpretation of the star of Bethlehem, demythologizing the accounts of natural events surrounding the death of Jesus does not undermine its significance. As stated in the

"Introduction," new cosmological insights require new understandings of theology. Believers maintain that Jesus was much more than a great man. He was the messiah, the Son of God. How are these statements of faith to be explained? Jesus's earliest followers had popular cosmological literary explanations at their disposal that would cast him in majestic roles recognizable to all. Contemporary followers do not understand those explanations literally. This does not mean that they do not believe. Both the accounts of the cosmic events at the time of Jesus's birth and those of upheavals of Earth at his death are metaphorical ways of claiming that something extraordinary has happened that can only be detected with the eyes of faith. Today's believers must devise ways of expressing this faith that are more in line with contemporary scientific thinking.

"The Son of God"

Most scholars hold that the central theme of the Gospel according to Mark is the identity of Jesus. Within that Gospel, with the exception of the Roman centurion who witnessed the extraordinary events at the death of Jesus, only unclean spirits recognize Jesus's true identity:

> Whenever the unclean spirits saw him, they fell down before him and shouted, "You are the Son of God!" (Mark 3:11)

and those possessed by an unclean spirit:

> And [the man with the unclean spirit] cried out, "What have you to do with us, Jesus of Nazareth? Have you come to destroy us? I know who you are, the Holy One of God." (Mark 1:24)

> And [the man possessed with an unclean spirit] shouted at the top of his voice, "What have you to do with me, Jesus, Son of the Most High God?" (Mark 5:7)

These unclean spirits might not be perceived, but the effects of their power over some people and the havoc they created could be:

Someone from the crowd answered him, "Teacher, I brought you my son; he has a spirit that makes him unable to speak; and whenever it seizes him, it dashes him down; and he foams and grinds his teeth and becomes rigid." (Mark 9:17–18)

And the unclean spirits came out and entered the swine; and the herd, numbering about two thousand, rushed down the steep bank into the sea, and were drowned in the sea. (Mark 5:13)

Why could these unclean spirits recognize Jesus's true identity and others could not, particularly those who witnessed his miracles? An understanding of miracles themselves will throw some light on the answer to that question.

Today, a miracle is generally thought to be an event that cannot be explained by scientific or natural causes. People in the Ancient Near East held a broader understanding of miracle. They recognized as divine activity many occurrences that we today would consider natural phenomena. In other words, where they saw something miraculous, we might see a marvelous event, but one that can be explained by the laws of nature. This is not to say that contemporary people do not believe that God is active in the world. It means, instead, that they recognize God's presence and activity through the agency of the phenomenon. It is a question of the difference between divine intervention with divine power being the direct or primary cause and God working through secondary causes.

More than any other Gospel, Mark portrays Jesus as a miracleworker. However, Mark does this not primarily to place Jesus in competition with the many miracleworkers of the day, but to portray him as the one whose wonders established the reign of God. The people at the time of Jesus believed that they were in the throes of a cosmic battle fought between the forces of good and the forces of evil.[5] They maintained that many of the evil forces made their presence and power known wherever the peace and prosperity promised by God were threatened or

---

[5] The final battles of this conflict are described in the Qumran scroll entitled "The War of the Sons of Light against the Sons of Darkness."

shattered. This was particularly evident in the case of disease, when demons were thought to have invaded human bodies, causing illness of every kind. These evil forces were often referred to as principalities or powers (see Rom 8:38; Col 1:16). In such situations it seemed that evil enjoyed a stronghold. Any act that demonstrated the power of God was seen as a victory over this controlling power of evil. The miracles of Jesus were perceived as actions that broke the evil power.[6] It is no wonder, then, that unclean spirits recognized Jesus's true identity. He threatened their authority and control.

This might explain the recognition by the unclean spirits, but why did the people who witnessed the marvelous event not come to the same conclusion? Some did, and some did not; some had faith, and others lacked it. Mark reports that a number of scribes claimed that the reason Jesus had power over the forces of evil was that he was aligned with them. In reply, Jesus insists that the kingdom he has come to establish is in opposition to the kingdom of evil, not an ally of it:

> And the scribes who came down from Jerusalem said, "He has Beelzebul, and by the ruler of the demons he casts out demons." And he called them to him, and spoke to them in parables, "How can Satan cast out Satan? If a kingdom is divided against itself, that kingdom cannot stand. And if a house is divided against itself, that house will not be able to stand. And if Satan has risen up against himself and is divided, he cannot stand, but his end has come." (Mark 3:22–26)

The very fact that people came or were brought to Jesus indicates that, while they might not have faith in him as Son of God, they believed in his power to heal them. In some passages faith plays a very significant role in the healing itself:

---

[6] The relationship between exorcisms and the inbreaking of the reign of God is explicitly stated in a passage from Luke: "But if it is by the finger of God that I cast out the demons, then the kingdom of God has come to you" (Luke 11:20).

> When Jesus saw their faith, he said to the
> paralytic,
> "Son, your sins are forgiven." (Mark 2:5)

He tells the woman with the hemorrhage:

> "Daughter, your faith has made you well; go
> in peace,
> and be healed of your disease." (Mark 5:34)

and Jairus who pleaded for the healing of his daughter:

> "Do not fear, only believe." (Mark 5:36)

and the blind Bartimaeus:

> "Go; your faith has made you well." (Mark
> 10:52)

Jesus chides his followers when they demonstrated a lack of faith when these seasoned fishermen were terrified by a storm at sea:

> "Why are you afraid? Have you still no
> faith?" (Mark 14:40)

and when they were unable to heal a boy possessed by an unclean spirit:

> "You faithless generation." (Mark 9:19)

The importance of even minimal faith is seen in Jesus's response to his rejection by the citizens of his own hometown:

> And he could do no deed of power there, except that he
> laid his hands on a few sick people and cured them. And
> he was amazed at their unbelief. (Mark 6:5–6a)

It is clear from these passages that faith was important. However, what was the nature of that faith? Were the people to believe in the power of the healing? Or in the power of the healer? If the first, then one might expect an external healing regardless of the nature or disposition of the healer. If the second, one would believe in the power and identity of the healer regardless of whether or not healing took place. Again, if these healings and exorcisms were primarily external wonders, why did not more people believe in Jesus's power and true identity?

According to Mark, Jesus not only cast out unclean spirits,[7] but he also performed many healings. He healed Peter's mother-in-law of a fever (1:29–31); a man of leprosy (1:40–42); a man of paralysis (2:1–12); a man of a withered hand (3:1–6); a woman of a hemorrhage (5:24–34); a man of deafness (7:31–37); and two men of blindness (8:22–25; 10:46–52). In addition, he brought a young girl back to life (5:21–23, 35–42). In each healing, Jesus restored to health an ailing human being, thus restoring to the embrace of community an afflicted person who earlier had been marginalized because of the ailment. Though these passages do not include reference to an exorcism, the cosmological worldview of the ancient Israelites included some demonic activity. If the invasion of someone's body by a demon resulted in illness, then an act of healing could be seen as a kind of exorcism. Thus, when Jesus performed an exorcism or a healing, the power of the demon was broken and the reign of God established. Human beings may not have always recognized God's power working through Jesus, but unclean spirits realized that they were losing their grip on the world. Their kingdom was crumbling, while the reign of God was being established.

The reports of two other very different miraculous events should be noted. They describe the power Jesus exercised over unruly water. In the first story (4:35–41) Jesus is asleep in a boat. Afraid that they, seasoned fishermen, will all be swallowed by the raging water, his disciples awaken him. He rebukes the wind and calms the sea. In the second account (6:47–52) the disciples are alone in a boat when the wind turns against them. Walking on the sea, Jesus appears to pass by them. Terrified, they cry out to him and he responds, "Take heart, it is I; do not be afraid." Elements in these stories are meant to show that Jesus is the

---

[7] Other exorcisms are found in Mark 1:32, 34, 39; 3:11; 5:2–8; and 7:24–30.

Son of God. An ancient Mesopotamia creation story tells of a young warrior-god defeating evil forces characterized as chaotic waters. This theme is found in some of the poetry of the Old Testament.[8] The idea developed that only the great Creator God could control unruly waters. Jesus's ability to do so was evidence of his divine identity. In the second account Jesus identifies himself: "It is I" (6:50). This is a very technical phrase. The Greek *égó eimi* (I, I am) has been variously translated: "I am he," or "I am who am," a reference to the self-identification of God to Moses through the burning bush (Exod 3:14). These two nature miracles clearly proclaim the divinity of Jesus.

Miracles present a complex challenge for anyone reading them through a lens fashioned by ecojustice principles. Historical, literary, and theological issues are involved. From the historical perspective one might ask: Did such wondrous events really happen? People at the time of Jesus, who espoused a dualistic worldview in which forces of good battled forces of evil, might easily answer yes. However, contemporary readers, who support an evolutive rather than a dualistic worldview, will say no. Might the stories be literary explanations rather than historical accounts? Even if one answers this question positively, such an answer does not offer a significantly different understanding, since the stories themselves presume a cosmic battle that is an element of the dualistic worldview. This difference might be compatible with the thinking of the early believers, but not with the thinking of today.

The theological issues are no less problematic. Fundamentally, miracles are manifestations of the power of God. Certainly, believers of all ages hold that divine power is at work in our world. This belief is not being challenged here. At issue is the manner of God's activity. Whether one holds that the stories are historical accounts or literary explanations, they still clearly point to the suspension of the laws of nature in favor of some form of divine intervention. In miracles God appears to disregard the intrinsic value of creation's inherent design and to refashion it for the sake of human beings. In this anthropocentric view the interconnectedness of the components of Earth is breached, and those components are forced to serve human goals.

---

[8] See, for example, Job 26:8–10; Psalms 29:3; 33:7; and Isaiah 28:2.

It may be that contemporary believers will have to relinquish the miracle as a viable way of perceiving the activity of God in the world. This does not mean that divine power can no longer exorcise or heal. It means, rather, that God accomplishes such restoration indirectly through medical procedures, human agency, or natural events. This way of understanding the miraculous requires that we be sensitive to the dynamic cosmic design of the world of which we are a part and that we assume our role in furthering the well-being of that world.

"Teacher"

Like Matthew's and Mark's Gospels, the Gospel according to Luke focuses on the identity of Jesus and discipleship. However, each Gospel provides a slightly different point of view. Matthew was written for a predominantly Jewish-Christian church; Mark is associated with Rome; and Luke was written for Gentile Christians. While all three Gospels portray Jesus as a teacher, Luke contains a major collection of his parables.

A parable is a metaphoric story intended to transform the perspective of those hearing it rather than to develop the ideas it contains. It is a word picture that, by means of comparison, describes something well known in order to throw light on something unfamiliar. Drawn from nature or common experience, the parable contains an unexpected twist meant to convince or surprise. It is a standard teaching device found in the Old Testament.[9] It shares many characteristics with proverbs, riddles, or allegories, pedagogical techniques employed by ancient Israel's sages. Thus, it is safe to say that in teaching through parables Jesus is depicted as a teacher in the tradition of ancient Israelite wisdom.

The parables of Luke emphasize many themes. Chief among them is the character of the reign of God. A look at a few parables illustrates this:

---

[9] The story told to David about the theft of a prized lamb (2 Sam 12:1–6) and the Song of the Vineyard (Isa 5:1–4) are recognized parables.

He said therefore, "What is the kingdom of God like? And to what should I compare it? It is like a mustard seed that someone took and sowed in the garden; it grew and became a tree, and the birds of the air made nests in its branches." And again he said, "To what should I compare the kingdom of God? It is like yeast that a woman took and mixed in with three measures of flour until all of it was leavened." (Luke 13:18–21)

Since a parable begins with what is known, a careful examination of the details of the story is the first step in understanding it. The parables in the passage above describe aspects of everyday life of both a man and a woman. Though the mustard seed in the first parable is traditionally known as one of the smallest of seeds, being linked with the parable of the yeast suggests that the gospel writer is less concerned with the size of the seed than with its potential for growth. Many commentators note that "birds of the air" is a reference to Gentiles. While this might be the case elsewhere, Gentile inclusion does not seem to be Luke's concern here, and so the reference might simply be to birds generally. The yeast in the second parable leavens the dough so that it expands.

Both the man and the woman perform very common acts—planting and kneading dough—and in doing so they engage rather insignificant elements, a seed and yeast. Emphasizing the character of these actions and elements makes a point about the reign of God. It is brought forward through very common acts, employing relatively insignificant elements. However, the growth or expansiveness of which they are capable is surprising and extraordinarily significant. So is the reign of God, brought forth through very common human actions, employing relatively insignificant components of Earth. Finally, in order for this growth or expansiveness to occur, the seed must decay and the yeast must ferment. Likewise, the reign of God calls for personal transformation. Old ways must be left behind so that newness can burst forth.

These parables illustrate Luke's knowledge and appreciation of the mysteries of the potential for growth hidden within Earth and the components of Earth. The intrinsic integrity of these mysteries functions as a sign or symbol of the mysteries of the reign of God. Were this not the case, the parable's metaphoric comparison would be empty and the power of its theological message would be lost.

Observing the patterns of life and growth in the natural world over the years has enabled human beings to anticipate seasonal changes. They can rely on this natural order to establish a degree of order in human life and society. As seen in the previous chapter, the very dependability of this natural order was employed by the sages of ancient Israel to teach various lessons. As a teacher in this Wisdom tradition, Jesus adopted this pedagogical technique:

> So he told them this parable: "Which one of you, having a hundred sheep and losing one of them, does not leave the ninety-nine in the wilderness and go after the one that is lost until he finds it? When he has found it, he lays it on his shoulders and rejoices. And when he comes home, he calls together his friends and neighbors, saying to them, 'Rejoice with me, for I have found my sheep that was lost.' Just so, I tell you, there will be more joy in heaven over one sinner who repents than over ninety-nine righteous persons who need no repentance.
>
> Or what woman having ten silver coins, if she loses one of them, does not light a lamp, sweep the house, and search carefully until she finds it? When she has found it, she calls together her friends and neighbors, saying, 'Rejoice with me, for I have found the coin that I had lost.' Just so, I tell you, there is joy in the presence of the angels of God over one sinner who repents." (Luke 15:3–10)

This set of parables, like the previous set, describes circumstances to which men can relate, as well as a situation from the lives of women. In the first parable the shepherd knows which sheep can be trusted to remain where he leaves them so that he can go after the one gone astray. Such understanding can only grow out of familiarity with and respect for the strengths, abilities, and unique characteristics of each member of the flock. Contrary to what some have said, the behavior of the shepherd does not suggest that the one wayward sheep is more important than the ninety-nine others. It means, instead, that each animal has value in itself and that the shepherd is willing to inconvenience himself for the sake of that one sheep. Many commentators think that the coin for which the woman searches is part of the elaborate wedding headdress, popular in the Ancient Near East. However, the parable is not concerned with the exact nature of the coin but with its value. The Greek word translated here as "coin" is *drachma*, the value of which might be equivalent to a day's wages.

Both parables speak of rejoicing in finding what was lost. However, the rejoicing stems from the fact that what was lost was considered to be of inestimable value. It was not viewed as one among many, easily replaced. Quite the contrary. Things of earth are valuable in themselves. This is seen in the way the searches were conducted. The one searching was single-minded in that search, not willing to settle for the reliable ninety-nine other sheep or the secure nine coins. This detail in the stories is important for the theological point made by the parables, namely, that each individual is important in itself, whether sheep, coin, or sinner. Furthermore, their importance is such that they are unreservedly sought by the shepherd, by the woman, and by God. What was lost did not reinstate itself; it was found, and its having been found was joyously celebrated.

In another well-known comparison story Jesus points to components of Earth as sources of insight for human beings:

> Consider the ravens: they neither sow nor reap, they have neither storehouse nor barn, and yet God feeds them. Of how much more value are you than the birds! And can any of you by worrying add a single hour to your span of life? If then you are not able to do so small a thing as that, why do you worry about the rest? Consider the lilies, how they grow: they neither toil nor spin; yet I tell you, even Solomon in all his glory was not clothed like one of these. But if God so clothes the grass of the field, which is alive today and tomorrow is thrown into the oven, how much more will he clothe you—you of little faith! (Luke 12:24–28)

The Greek work translated "consider" means "study, draw a lesson from." The ravens and the lilies have something to teach Jesus's followers. The ravens do not plan their survival, nor do the flowers design the splendor in which they are garbed. They simply live faithful to their natures, and God provides. Human beings should learn from this. While planning and designing might be natural to humans, anxiety should not be. The argument moves from what is considered light to what is heavy or more important. The ravens might be considered of negligible importance because they are scavengers and therefore unclean. The beauty of the lily is short lived; it soon fades and the flower dies. If God cares for unclean birds and the fleeting beauty of what grows out of Earth, how much more will God care for people?

This passage suggests that human beings are valued more than other creatures of Earth. However, this preference does not stand in opposition to the ecojustice principle of intrinsic value, for the importance of human beings in no way detracts from the care God bestows on the ravens or the lilies. In fact, this apparent hierarchy of importance corresponds to the principle of purpose that states: "Earth and all its components are part of a dynamic cosmic design within which each piece has a place in the overall goal of that design."[10] As scavengers, ravens rid the locale in which they live of carrion that might spread disease. Lilies add beauty and fragrance to their surroundings. They contribute to their respective ecosystems whether human beings are there or not. Thus, their value is neither determined by human beings nor diminished by their dignity. Only by living in accord with their nature do all the components of Earth contribute to the goal of that design.

"The Bread of Life"

The Gospel according to John presents a very different profile of Jesus from that of the Synoptic Gospels. It does not open with an infancy narrative or stories about the beginning of his ministry, but with an identification of him as the eternal Word of God. Here Jesus exorcises no demons, tells no parables. Instead, he delivers long symbolic discourses and attaches symbolic meaning

---

[10] Norman C. Habel, ed., *The Earth Bible*, vol. 1, *Readings from the Perspective of Earth* (Cleveland: The Pilgrim Press, 2000), 24.

to the few healings he performs. In this Gospel his miracles are signs providing glimpses into his true identity and are meant to evoke faith on the part of those who witness them. Literary and theological features of this Gospel have led scholars to date it much later than Matthew, Mark, and Luke, at a time when the early Christians were developing a rather sophisticated Christology. Here Jesus identifies himself through "I am" sayings: "I am the light of the world" (8:12); "I am the gate" (10:9); "I am the good shepherd" (10:11); "I am the resurrection and the life" (11:25); "I am the way, and the truth, and the life" (14:6); "I am the true vine" (15:1). In each case he explains how eternal life will come only through him.

In the discourse that follows John's account of the feeding of the multitude, Jesus proclaims: "I am the bread of life" (6:35). This story can be divided into three parts: the feeding itself (6:4–14), the theological meaning of the feeding (6:32–33), and Jesus's identification of himself (6:35, 41, 48–51, 53–58).

> Now the Passover, the festival of the Jews, was near. When he looked up and saw a large crowd coming toward him, Jesus said to Philip, "Where are we to buy bread for these people to eat?" He said this to test him, for he himself knew what he was going to do. Philip answered him, "Six months' wages would not buy enough bread for each of them to get a little." One of his disciples, Andrew, Simon Peter's brother, said to him, "There is a boy here who has five barley loaves and two fish. But what are they among so many people?" Jesus said, "Make the people sit down." Now there was a great deal of grass in the place; so they sat down, about five thousand in all. Then Jesus took the loaves, and when he had given thanks, he distributed them to those who were seated; so also the fish, as much as they wanted. When they were satisfied, he told his disciples, "Gather up the fragments left over, so that nothing may be lost." So they gathered them up, and from the fragments of the five barley loaves, left by those who had eaten, they filled twelve baskets. When the people saw the sign that he had done, they began to say, "This is indeed the prophet who is to come into the world." (John 6:4–14)

The feeding of the multitude is the only miracle story that is found in all of the Gospels (cf. Matt 14:13–21; 15:34–39; Mark 6:35–44; 8:1–10; and Luke 9:10–17). While the version in John enjoys many of the literary characteristics found in the Synoptic Gospels, few scholars believe that this evangelist was influenced by one of the earlier Gospels. They maintain, instead, that he was working from an earlier source, perhaps the same source used by the other gospel writers. In any case, John is less interested in the historical reliability of the account than in its theological meaning.

There are, in fact, several different yet interrelated levels of theological meaning. First, the story must be understood within the context and meaning of the feast of Passover, indicated in the biblical text itself (v. 4). The bread is identified as barley loaves. This too suggests Passover, which was the festival that originated as the celebration of the barley harvest. Second, the multiplication of loaves calls to mind the account of a similar miracle performed by Elisha. There the prophet directed his servant to feed a hundred people with five barley loaves and fresh ears of corn. The leftovers of that meal were also gathered up (see 2 Kgs 4:42–44). Third, a eucharistic hint is found in the verb for "given thanks" *(eucharistésas)*. Finally, there is an eschatological dimension to this story. While the two fish may have simply been dried or pickled fish often eaten with bread, this detail calls to mind the tradition that at the endtime, the time of fulfillment, the chaotic monsters of the deep, Leviathan and Behemoth, will be eaten at the glorious messianic banquet. Furthermore, amazed by this miraculous feeding, the people wonder whether Jesus might be "the prophet who is to come into the world," an eschatological reference to a messianic figure.

In the story Jesus walks across the turbulent Sea of Galilee to Capernaum. The next day, in response to the people's request for more bread, Jesus begins his explanation of the miracle:

> Then Jesus said to them, "Very truly, I tell you, it was not Moses who gave you the bread from heaven, but it is my Father who gives you the true bread from heaven. For the bread of God is that which comes down from heaven and gives life to the world." (John 6:32–33)

With this reference to the manna with which the people were fed in the wilderness (Exod 16), Jesus focuses first on an aspect of the Passover theme. Because they did nothing to produce that bread, the ancient Israelites considered this manna "bread from heaven."[11] Jesus corrects their misperception. The manna was not really bread from heaven. Rather, the bread that God gives is the true bread from heaven. Jesus then declares: "I am the bread of life" (v. 35) and "I have come down from heaven" (v. 38). In this way he argues that he, as the true bread from heaven, gives life to the world.

After a short explanation of his relationship with God, which enables him to grant eternal life to those united with him (vv. 43–47), Jesus contrasts the inadequacy of the manna with the power that is his as the true bread that came down from heaven:

> "I am the bread of life. Your ancestors ate the manna in the wilderness, and they died. This is the bread that comes down from heaven, so that one may eat of it and not die. I am the living bread that came down from heaven. Whoever eats of this bread will live forever; and the bread that I will give for the life of the world is my flesh." (John 6:48–51)

In addition to the Passover theme seen in the reference to the manna, a new theme is introduced by the word "flesh" *(sarx)*. While most eucharistic references use the word "body" *(sóma)*, the use of this term links the Eucharist with the death of Jesus. The promise of eternal life picks up the eschatological theme.

The entire discourse ends with the eschatological promise that flows from eucharistic theology:

> So Jesus said to them, "Very truly, I tell you, unless you eat the flesh of the Son of Man and drink his blood, you have no life in you. Those who eat my flesh and drink my blood have eternal life, and I will raise them up on the last day; for my flesh is true food and my blood is true drink.

---

[11] Manna comes Hebrew *ma hû'*, which means "what is it?" It probably came from drippings of the tamarisk tree, which dried into an edible, flaky substance.

Those who eat my flesh and drink my blood abide in me, and I in them. Just as the living Father sent me, and I live because of the Father, so whoever eats me will live because of me. This is the bread that came down from heaven, not like that which your ancestors ate, and they died. But the one who eats this bread will live forever." (John 6:53–58)

The bread that was originally considered nourishment essential for survival (manna) has been replaced by true bread (bread from heaven). This bread from heaven becomes both a sign of divine providence (life to the world) and a promise of eschatological fulfillment (eternal life). Jesus's claim of being the true bread from heaven means that eschatological fulfillment comes through union with him ("eat my flesh"). This is accomplished first through the physical sacrifice of his flesh and then the eucharistic sharing of that flesh through the eating of this true bread from heaven.

Throughout this very complex weaving of theological themes one issue stands out unambiguously as of primary importance. That issue is the indispensability of bread for life, whether to physical life on earth or eternal life as union with God. If bread was not in itself essential, it would not carry such importance as a sign and a promise. Though bread is not a fundamental element of Earth, it is made of the fruits of Earth for one and only one purpose, the sustaining and furthering of life. Within this biblical tradition, as manna, bread symbolizes divine providence; as wisdom, it represents the sustenance of truth; as the flesh of Jesus, it is the extent to which he is willing to give himself; as the Eucharist, it is the means of our union with God. In each case human beings are dependent on the bread; the bread does not rely on human beings for its importance.

The Imitation of Christ

The road to Christian formation and discipleship has often been called "the imitation of Christ." A popular contemporary phrase asks: What would Jesus do? This might sound deceptively simple until one realizes that the only portraits we have of Jesus are the Gospels, and these Gospels are not historically precise accounts of events or detailed descriptions of people involved in those events. Furthermore, these accounts themselves grew out of perceptions and understandings grounded in a worldview very different from the one held by today's women and men. So, it is not easy to know what Jesus would do.

A literal imitation of Christ raises some important cosmological questions. For example: How does one imitate a first-century Jewish miracleworker when one believes that the goal of the dynamic cosmic design is broader than merely the physical or spiritual healing of human beings? Put another way, how might one model one's actions after Jesus when one maintains that God works wonders through the laws and processes of nature rather than through miraculous intervention, as the Gospel stories suggest? This is not to say that one cannot imitate Jesus's behavior. Rather, it means that one cannot be satisfied merely with what these stories say but must discover what they mean, and that meaning must be expressed in ways that can be accepted by the contemporary world. In other words, simple retrieval and interpretation of a gospel passage are not enough. One must interpret, sometime even reinterpret, that passage for a contemporary context.

One of the methods of reinterpretation employed in this chapter has been demythologization. This is a process of explaining cosmic phenomena using scientific principles rather than mythical categories. The insights gained from this approach show that divine majesty manifests itself through the unpretentious elements of Earth, rather than as an invincible demonstration of power and might that sets aside the laws governing these elements. This underscores the ecojustice principle of intrinsic value of the elements of Earth. As shown above, demythologizing the accounts of the Christmas star, the miracles of Jesus, and the darkness and earthquake at his death does not deny the power of God working through natural forces or through Jesus himself. Rather, it calls us to understand the working of this power in a different way. This means that the religious message of these accounts can be retrieved, but it must be reinterpreted and expressed in contemporary ways. This demythologizing approach reaffirms the sense of catholicity, the ancient Greek concept of a universal physical order spoken of so often in this series. Finally, maintaining that God works through the laws and forces of nature actually suggests that even God respects the integrity of creation.

As interpreted above, the healing narratives point to the dawning of the reign of God, a theme that grew out of the religious expectations of ancient Israel, but which touches an aspect of the contemporary notion of an evolving universe. The Bible characterizes this eschatological notion of the dawning of the reign of God as somehow temporal. It seems to be a kind of linear movement—this age and the age to come. There is only a suggestion of this openness to a very different future in these healing accounts. We will have to wait until an examination of the teaching of Paul and the vision in Revelation to see how this evolving future is perceived.

"One untimely born"

—1 Corinthians 15:8

Chapter Six

In the history of Christianity, Paul's importance is second only to that of Jesus. Though his theology has been systematized by other theologians down through the centuries, Paul himself was a practical theologian, one who developed theology out of the experience of life rather than from within a philosophical framework. This explains why there is both repetition and often significant diversity in his teaching. He spoke to the actual concerns and struggles of the various people to whom he proclaimed the good news of Jesus Christ. As he did this, he drew on aspects of their world of understanding. This included fundamental Jewish thought as well as various Hellenist concepts.

Paul was a Hellenistic Jew, born in Tarsus, Cilicia, what is today the southern coast of Turkey (Acts 22:3).[1] A tentmaker by trade (Acts 18:3), he was educated at the feet of the great Jewish scholar Gamaliel, yet he quoted scripture from the Greek Septuagint. He possessed basic Hellenistic rhetorical skills, as evidenced in the character of the letters he left behind. He was a man of great passion, which first prompted him to persecute the followers of Jesus; their teaching, he maintained, had debased the ancient religious tradition of Israel (Acts 22:4). While on a

---

[1] The historical accuracy of the details found in Acts of the Apostles is questioned by many. However, the information in these biblical stories forms a traditional picture of the early community of the followers of Jesus.

journey to Damascus where he planned to capture Christians and bring them back to Jerusalem for trial and punishment, he had a revelatory experience of the risen Jesus that totally transformed him from a fierce persecutor to an avid disciple. Paul took no credit for this transformation. In fact, he refers to it as being "untimely born" (1 Cor 15:8). The Greek word used *(éktroma)* means "unnatural or violent birth," "miscarriage," even "abortion." By using such an offensive word, Paul emphasized his initial resistance to God's designs for him and the violence that marked his entrance into the life of a believer. However, once born, he redirected his zeal from being vehemently against to being single-mindedly committed to Jesus and his message of salvation.

Paul availed himself of the system of Roman roads that connected the provinces, enabling him to traverse the empire in his desire to proclaim the gospel to the whole world. As he moved from place to place, he remained in contact with the converts he made in the various cities by writing messages. Paul's own letters, and several that were written by his disciples but attributed to him, formed the basis of the theology of the early church.

In many ways the theology that Paul taught was grounded in the truth of Jesus's resurrection. Thus, he argued that if Jesus had not been raised from the dead, "vain is our faith" (1 Cor 15:14). As a Pharisee (Phil 3:5), he believed in resurrection. Based on this faith in Jesus's resurrection, he developed his Christology (understanding of the true nature of Jesus), his soteriology (theology of salvation), his eschatology (belief in a future time of fulfillment), and his understanding of Christian identity.

Literary Context

Of the twenty-seven books of the New Testament, thirteen are somehow associated with Paul. Though these writings have been variously referred to as either letters or epistles, strict distinctions between these two literary forms have been made. The classical Greek epistle was an artistic literary form of instruction meant for a general, public audience. The format was quite standard. It opened with an introductory salutation that identified both the sender and the audience. This was followed by words of thanksgiving for blessings already received from the gods. Next came the body of the letter containing the reason or reasons for writing. The closing included a wish for good health, greetings to notables in the audience, and a form of benediction. A letter, on the other hand, was an informal means of communication. Though it might contain some of the elements of the formal epistle, it was written to a particular individual or group, and it addressed a specific issue.

Paul's writings cannot be easily classified as one form rather than the other. While they contain many of the features of the formal epistle, they were really letters written to specific individuals or groups of believers and were probably not meant for the general public. Only much later were these written communications collected and circulated among the various Christian communities as general teaching for the entire early church. Scholars today maintain that not all of the letters were actually written by Paul.[2] Letters whose Pauline authorship is not questioned include 1 Thessalonians, Galatians, Philippians, 1 and 2 Corinthians, Romans, and Philemon. Those referred to as Deutero-Pauline are 2 Thessalonians, Colossians, and Ephesians. Scholars agree on the pseudonymous authorship of 1 and 2 Timothy and Titus. Though the authorship of several of these letters is questioned, their status as sacred scripture with revelatory value is not. The early Christians considered the content of each one of these letters important for their understanding of the good news that Paul or his followers preached.

Besides being categorized according to authorship, the letters are also classified according to content. Philippians, Philemon, Colossians, and Ephesians are called captivity letters, because in them the author refers to his imprisonment. Titus and 1 and 2 Timothy provide directions for the establishment of church structures and discipline and, therefore, are called pastoral letters.

Birthpangs of Creation

Paul's Letter to the Romans is the longest of his letters and is considered the most important. It was probably written from

---

[2] Not all of Paul's letters have been handed down to us. Both 1 Corinthians 5:9 and 2 Corinthians 2:3 refer to letters we do not have.

the vicinity of Cenchreae, the port for the city of Corinth, around 55–58 CE. Unlike the recipients of the other genuine Pauline letters, the Christians in Rome had not heard the good news from Paul himself. This explains why this letter lacks the familiarity found in many of his other writings. References to Jewish faith and practice lay bare the Jewish-Christian character of this community. Many scholars believe that it was founded by Jewish-Christians from Jerusalem who came to the imperial city precisely to make converts to the Christian faith. By the time Paul wrote the letter, the community consisted of both Jewish and Gentile Christians. Convinced that he had completed his missionary work in the eastern Mediterranean area, Paul turned his eyes to the West, specifically to Spain (Rom 15:24). From his point of view, Rome promised to be a profitable base for his projected travels.

Scholars are in agreement regarding the importance of the theme of salvation in this letter. However, there are several ways in which that theme might be understood. Salvation certainly was a prominent issue in the Greco-Roman gnostic philosophy of the time, and some scholars maintain that this was the source of Paul's understanding of the concept. However, Paul had been educated at the feet of Gamaliel (Acts 22:3), one of the most prominent Jewish thinkers of the day. One can conclude from this that Paul was well versed in Jewish apocalyptic eschatological thinking.[3] While he does employ various gnostic concepts, principally the body-spirit distinction, it is clear that he was more influenced by Jewish apocalyptic thinking than the gnosticism of his time.

Jewish apocalypticism was a way of understanding history. Unlike gnosticism, which maintained that perfection would take place only when the material (body) was made subject to the immaterial (spirit), Jewish apocalypticism taught that transformation had less to do with the makeup of the human being than with the course of human history. It insisted that some form of total transformation would usher in a new age of existence,

---

[3] A major source of information about Jewish apocalyptic thinking of the time is Paul J. Achtemeier, *Romans, Interpretation: A Bible Commentary for Teaching and Preaching* (Atlanta: John Knox Press, 1985), 7–9.

and this transformation would include both material and immaterial aspects of the human person. Like the prophets, Jewish apocalyptic thinkers believed that God is in control of events, bringing to fulfillment the divine promises made to the ancestors. When it became obvious that many of these promises had not yet been fulfilled and might never be realized, the people were faced with a serious dilemma: Should they relinquish any hope of fulfillment, or should they refashion their understanding of fulfillment and the era within which fulfillment would take place?

Out of disappointment, some Jewish people probably chose the first option. Others clung to their belief that God would eventually bring the promises to fulfillment, and they reinterpreted their understanding. In doing so, they opted for an apocalyptic view of history, a view already found in earlier Jewish tradition (Isa 24—27; Ezek 38—39; Zech 12—14; Dan 7), and they ascribed extraordinary characteristics to a future age when God's promises would be fulfilled.

First and foremost, apocalypticism taught that a radical separation exists between the present time and the age to come. It taught that the present age of evil and destruction would be replaced by the new age of universal goodness and happiness. At that time, world history as it is presently known will give way to the reign of God. The Jewish apocalyptic tradition further taught that a period of suffering and purification would precede the full dawning of the new age or time of fulfillment. Paul's writing reflects this Jewish apocalyptic eschatology, particularly in an important passage from the Letter to the Romans:

> I consider that the sufferings of this present time are not worth comparing with the glory about to be revealed to us. For the creation waits with eager longing for the revealing of the children of God; for the creation was subjected to futility, not of its own will but by the will of the one who subjected it, in hope that the creation itself will be set free from its bondage to decay and will obtain the freedom of the glory of the children of God. We know that the whole creation has been groaning in labor pains until now; and not only the creation, but we ourselves, who have the first fruits of the Spirit, groan inwardly while we wait for adoption, the redemption of our bodies. (Rom 8:18–23)

The very first verse of this passage is rich in theological meaning. It sets the context within which the entire passage is to be understood. The Greek verb that introduces it, *logízomai* (I consider), indicates that what follows is an authoritative pronouncement. The eschatological character of this pronouncement is marked by *kairós*, a word translated as "time." Unlike *chrónos*, which refers to consecutive or unfolding time, *kairós* designates a special time, a time pregnant with extraordinary meaning. *Kairós* took on theological meaning and came to signify that future time of fulfillment. Paul uses this word to characterize the present, the time within which he and his readers were living. Thus, he is ascribing eschatological significance to the time in which he lived. This was an extraordinary claim.

The sufferings of which Paul speaks are not identified. The Christians could have been experiencing some form of oppression or persecution, or the suffering might have been caused by their struggle to reform their lives, or they could have been the vicissitudes of life that everyone has to face. Whatever the case, Paul had earlier in the letter exhorted his readers to join their suffering with the suffering of Christ (Rom 8:17). If Paul claims that the time in which they are living is the time of fulfillment, then the sufferings they are experiencing could also somehow be related to that extraordinary time. Paul clearly understands it in this way for he refers to these sufferings as the "birthpangs of the Messiah." While the word *birthpangs* is not explicitly mentioned in verse 18, it does appear in verse 22, allowing us to consider the sufferings referred to here as bearing eschatological significance. Understood in this way, the glory that is about to be revealed should also be seen as eschatological, not viewed as a reward for having endured suffering. It is clear that this glory does not belong by right to those who suffer. Rather, it belongs to Christ. As the previous verse stated, those who share in Christ's suffering will share in his glory. Since the context is apocalyptic eschatology, one can understand Christ's suffering and death apocalyptically, as the "birthpangs of the Messiah." One can thus conclude that his suffering and death have inaugurated the new age of fulfillment. This means that those joined to Christ in eschatological suffering will also enjoy eschatological glory.

In this passage the focus of the transformation is not primarily on human beings. It is on the created world. This is made quite clear by the appearance of the word *creation* in each of verses 19–23. While Paul seems here to distinguish between the rest of the natural world and the children of God (v. 19), he sees creation's intimate link with human beings in the futility and bondage that it endures and the freedom for which it "waits with eager longing." Most commentators maintain that behind the reference to creation's "bondage to decay" is the tradition of the punishment for the first sin, where the man is told: "Cursed is the ground because of you" (Gen 3:17).

It might at first appear that the innocent ground is unfairly made to suffer because of the sin of the first human couple. However, according to the ecoprinciple of interconnectedness, all members of the community of Earth both benefit from and suffer the consequences of the actions of one another. The Greek verbs used to describe this suffering reinforce this connection, in English, "groan together" and "suffer labor pangs together" (Rom 8:22). This notion is more than an instance of the use of apocalyptic imagery. Today, we have come to understand this interconnectedness in new ways; we realize that we are one with creation and that we share a common fate with all members of the community of Earth. Therefore, it is correct to say that our bondage is creation's bondage, and our transformation is creation's transformation.

It is also important to realize that Paul interprets the suffering of the Christians as birth pains, not death pains. Understood apocalyptically, this suffering is a passageway into transformation, not simply a punishment for transgression. Paul refers to this transformation as "adoption, the redemption of our bodies" (Rom 8:23). Adoption as children of God is yet another prominent concept found in the Jewish apocalyptic eschatological tradition. In that tradition believers are called children of God, and they are said to inherit the promises made by God, but not yet fulfilled.[4] Paul says that, as sons and daughters, they can now expect to enjoy the fulfillment of those promises in their own time.

The expression "redemption of our bodies" might be considered as an example of gnostic thinking. A careful look at the way Paul employs that word shows that while he uses the language

---

[4] See non-canonical writings 1 Enoch 62:11; Jubilees 1:24–25; 2:20; 4 Ezra 6:58.

of gnosticism, he has reinterpreted its meaning. Throughout his writing he often uses two Greek words interchangeably, *sóma* (body) and *sarx* (flesh). While these words carry similar meanings, they also denote very different ideas. *Sóma* has a broader meaning, frequently referring to the entire person, including both material and immaterial aspects. *Sarx* is more specific, denoting the fleshy, corporeal dimension of the human being. When Paul speaks about human weakness, he usually uses *sarx*. However, in his teaching about resurrection, *sóma* is normally used. Consequently, it is safe to say that when Paul here speaks of the "redemption of our bodies" *(sóma)*, he is talking about the transformation of the whole person, not merely the victory of an alleged superior spirit over a presumed inferior body, as the Gnostics might claim. Finally, this transformation of the whole person is expected at the time of eschatological fulfillment.

Just as creation groans in labor pains, so human beings too "groan inwardly" (Rom 8:23). Paul further states that despite—or perhaps because of—this groaning, human beings have the first fruits of the Spirit. First fruits is an agricultural concept. It signifies the very first growth of the harvest, which was thought to be the best and the most vital yield. Because of its value, the first fruits were considered the most appropriate part of the harvest to be offered to God. First fruits also suggest that there will be future growth, thus adding an eschatological dimension to the concept. In this passage the first fruits are not agricultural. They are "first fruits of the Spirit." The Greek form of expression allows various translations. Some commentators hold that the expression refers to the Spirit itself. Others understand it to mean fruits or gifts of the Spirit. What is important for the discussion here is the fact that believers already possess something of the Spirit, something that also promises future growth.

It is clear from the above explanation that Paul may have employed ideas also found in gnostic thought, but he developed his theology out of the context of Jewish apocalyptic eschatology rather than Hellenistic philosophic thinking. Moreover, he reinterpreted even the Jewish tradition to fit his own understanding of the role that Christ plays in the lives of believers, and indeed in the dynamic of the entire creation. While Paul retains the idea of two ages, he argues that there is actually an overlapping of these two eras. The death and resurrection of Jesus have inaugurated the new age of fulfillment or reign of God. However, that age or reign has not yet fully transformed the entire world. According to Paul, this will occur when Christ returns at the end of time (1 Cor 15:24). Therefore, the time of fulfillment has already come but is not yet complete. Hence the expression used by many New Testament scholars: *already-but-not-yet.*

This already-but-not-yet character is obvious in the passage under consideration. Paul's insistence on present fulfillment is seen in his identification of the believers as children of God (Rom 8:19) who already enjoy "the first fruits of the Spirit" (8:23). Anticipation of a jubilant future (not-yet) is expressed in every verse of this passage: "the glory about to be revealed"; "eager longing"; "in hope"; "will obtain . . . freedom"; "groaning in labor pains"; "first fruits"; and "we await" (Rom 8:18–23).

Some ecosensitive readers might find creation's sense of futility, its bondage to decay, and its groaning in pain (Rom 8:20–22) as disturbing evidence of a disregard of creation's voice in the face of injustice. However, such an attitude overlooks another ecojustice principle—interconnectedness. While interconnectedness subjects the natural world to the sufferings brought on by human failing, it also opens it to the eschatological transformation promised by God.[5] This participation in ultimate transformation is evidence of the presence of the first ecojustice principle—the acknowledgment of creation's intrinsic value.

The Firstborn of Creation

Colossae was an inland city of ancient Anatolia in Asia Minor, east of Ephesus, in what is today Turkey. Though Paul preached in the vicinity of the Lycus, the river on which the city was located, it appears that he never visited the city itself (Col 2:1). It is also possible that the people of Colossae heard of Paul and were converted to the good news of Jesus Christ through the preaching of Epaphras, a member of that community and a

---

[5] One is reminded of a child's innocent query about his dog being in heaven, and Pope Francis's simple reply that God loves all creation.

close disciple of Paul (1:7; 4:12). This letter, written in the late 60s CE,[6] sought to correct false teaching to which the people of Colossae had fallen victim. The false teaching appears to have been a syncretistic mix of various religious and philosophical concepts derived from Greek, Roman, Asian, and Jewish thought. This mix included aspects of astrology (the cult of astral deities), gnosticism (a philosophy that shunned the material world in favor of a spiritual world), mystery religions (religious groups with secret initiation and ritual practices know only to members), and Hellenistic Judaism.

The false teaching to which the Christians of Colossae had succumbed challenged the adequacy of Christ's salvific power. It claimed that elemental spirits of the universe existed that rivaled his power (Col 1:16) and that these angelic spirits could only be appeased through the exercise of certain ascetical practices (Col 2:16–19). Such astrological cults promised their devotees that if they were faithful to prescribed practices they would be released from the imprisonment in the body and thus be able to enjoy life in the higher realms of the spirit. It was to such cosmological errors that Paul addressed his magnificent christological hymn:[7]

> He is the image of the invisible God, the firstborn of all creation; for in him all things in heaven and on earth were created, things visible and invisible, whether thrones or dominions or rulers or powers—all things have been created through him and for him. He himself is before all things, and in him all things hold together. He is the head of the body, the church; he is the beginning, the firstborn from the dead, so that he might come to have first place in everything. For in him all the fullness of God was pleased to dwell, and through him God was pleased to reconcile to himself all things, whether on earth or in heaven, by making peace through the blood of his cross. (Col 1:15–20)

The imagery found in this hymn and the arguments made here offer clues to the errors that the author is challenging. The various

---

[6] Some commentators date this writing as late as the 80s CE.

[7] Though Paul is probably not the author of this letter, the traditional practice of ascribing authorship to him is followed here.

descriptions of Christ are all meant to show that the astral deities proposed by the false teachers cannot rival Christ's excellence.

Christ is first identified as "the image of the invisible God." This title consists of two very important yet seemingly contradictory concepts: image and invisible. An image, by definition, is a visible representation of something. When Paul states that God is invisible, he is insisting that God is not like the corporeal, half human–half divine deities revered by so many adherents of the current Eastern religions. Rather, God is a spiritual being, not limited by physical dimensions. Identifying Christ as the image of the invisible God, Paul claims that Christ makes visible this God who is in essence invisible. But how does this occur? An understanding of how the word *image* is understood in the Bible can help to answer that question.

Image immediately calls to mind the creation tradition, in which the first man and woman were made "in the image of God" (Gen 1:27). In the Ancient Near East an image was not seen as a pattern according to which copies were made. Nor was an image of a god an idol that was worshiped. Rather, an image was a unique, symbolic, material representation of the authority of a deity. It signaled the place where that deity ruled supreme. At times the people's devotion might have deteriorated into ascribing divine significance to the image itself, thus resulting in their worshiping it as an idol. However, such a situation would have been a failure in understanding the image as a symbol of the deity, not as part of its essence. The image actually functioned in the way a national flag might function today, designating localized power, authority, and jurisdiction. In the Genesis account the commission to "subdue . . . and have dominion" (Gen 1:28) identifies the activities in which the man and the woman are to act as God's image, in God's stead, in a way that God would act.[8] The human beings were not gods, free to exercise this power, authority, and jurisdiction any way they pleased. They might have had a special relationship with God

---

[8] Since it was God's creative will that living beings flourish (Gen 1:11, 20, 24), the commission to "subdue . . . and have dominion" (language that characterizes the man and woman as royalty) places on the human couple the responsibility to ensure that life is protected and that it thrive.

that authorized them to represent God, but they themselves were subject to God's authority. Their attempt to act as gods resulted in their sin and subsequent punishment (Genesis 3). Identifying Christ as the image of God, Paul is saying that Christ enjoys a special relationship with God that authorizes him to represent God and to function in God's stead, as God would function. The verse itself does not identify the nature of that relationship or the scope of Christ's activity as image of God. However, this will be made clear in the following verses of the passage.

Paul next identifies Christ as "the firstborn of all creation." While *firstborn* could refer to the first in chronological order, in the biblical tradition it is a designation of privilege. The firstborn is the one who inherits the birthright of the family along with the bulk of its property and holdings. In this way the firstborn is the linchpin within the kinship structure, assuring that this kinship will survive and linking ancestors with descendants. In other words the firstborn enjoys primacy of function within the kinship structure, not merely primacy of place.

Paul states that Christ is the "firstborn of all creation," not simply of humankind. The focus here is not on his relationship with the rest of the human race but with the entire cosmos. The concept calls to mind the ancient Israelite tradition of Wisdom personified as found in Proverbs, the Wisdom of Solomon, and Sirach. This mysterious figure, who clearly comes from God, has an important role to play in creation. Wisdom herself declares:

> The LORD created me at the beginning of his work, the first of his acts of long ago. Ages ago I was set up, at the first, before the beginning of the earth. (Prov 8:22–23; see Wis 9:9; Sir 1:4)

In the verses that follow in this passage from Proverbs, Wisdom describes herself as having been present when the rest of creation was formed and established. She then very boldly claims that she was there at the time of creation as more than a spectator:

> Then I was beside him, like a master worker. (Prov 8:30)[9]

---

[9] Though the Hebrew word is sometimes translated "little child," most commentators prefer "master worker" or "architect."

Wisdom implies here that, while God is definitely Creator, all things were somehow created through her. This idea was not unique to the tradition of Israel. The notion that God created through an intermediary was very popular in some of the philosophical thinking of Paul's day. Philo, the Hellenistic Jewish philosopher from Alexandria, Egypt, believed that God had a partner in creation, and he called that partner both Wisdom and Logos (word). In pre-Socratic philosophy the logos was the divine reason implicit in the cosmos, ordering the cosmos and giving it form and meaning. The people in Colossae, socialized in Greek thinking, would have been familiar with this concept. Therefore, they would have understood Paul's identification of Christ as "firstborn of creation."

The Wisdom tradition presumes that there is an underlying order in the universe that human beings must discover and to which they must conform their lives so that they might survive and thrive. This order is beyond the scope of human understanding or control. In this regard human beings are like all other members of the community of Earth, part of the order and dependent on other members of the community for growth and enhancement. This order corresponds to the ecojustice principle of purpose, which speaks of a "dynamic cosmic design within which each piece has a place in the overall goal of that design," as well as the principles of intrinsic worth and interconnectedness.[10]

Just as "image of the invisible God" signifies Christ's relationship with God, "firstborn" signifies Christ's relationship with the rest of creation. Linking these ideas together, as we find in the Letter to the Colossians, highlights the point that Paul is making. He believes that as image of God, Christ represents God in the very activity of creation and in that way Christ functions in God's stead. Colossians points to this understanding when it states: "For in him all things . . . were created" (Col 1:16). Lest there be any doubt regarding the all-inclusiveness of Christ's creative influence among "all things," Paul cites major categories of beings over which Christ exercises supremacy: things "in heaven and on earth, things visible and invisible." If all things

---

[10] Norman C. Habel, ed., *The Earth Bible*, vol. 1, *Readings from the Perspective of Earth* (Cleveland: The Pilgrim Press, 2000), 24.

were created in Christ, there certainly is an interconnectedness among "all things," an intrinsic catholicity.

To hold sway over the visible things of Earth is in itself a major feat. This kind of influence has been the dream of many conquerors down through the ages, even to our own day. To exercise that same influence over the invisible heavenly beings is another matter altogether. The Colossians would understand this to mean that the astral deities—referred to as thrones, dominions, rulers, and powers—so prominent in some of the religious cults of the day, were no match for Christ. He far surpassed them, for all of the cosmos was created through him, a claim that none of the other deities could make.

To say that "all things have been created through him" underscores the similar functioning in the activity of creation between Christ as firstborn and ancient Israel's preexistent Wisdom and philosophy's Logos. However, what follows in the Colossian letter is said only of Christ: "All things have been created through him and for him." This last statement makes Christ not only the agent of God through whom all is created, but also the very goal of creation. According to Paul, Christ is both the beginning and the end of all things. Furthermore, he is both preexistent and the power that holds all creation together, sustaining it and unifying it (Col 1:17), similar to but not identical with the Stoic concept of world-soul. All creation is united in and through Christ.

It is clear that Paul is talking about the risen Christ, not Jesus in his humanity. In other words, humanity is not the agent or goal of creation as radical anthropocentrism might suggest; it is not the beginning and end of all things. Paul does not divinize humanity, thus placing it over the rest of creation. He did not believe that the natural world was created for the sake of human beings and then given to them to do with it what they choose, as some people have claimed. Paul insisted that Christ's preeminence in these matters flows from his unique intimate relationship with God. Human beings can make no such claim.

The first verses of this hymn focus on Christ's sovereignty over all creation. Paul next turns to the idea of Christ's leadership over the church. As he sketches the outlines of Christ's relationship with the members of the church, he employs head-body imagery. The Colossians would have been familiar with this imagery, for Philo and other Hellenistic philosophers taught that the world was actually the body of a god and all created components of that world were parts of the body. Paul uses the body image in other letters (Rom 12:4–8; 1 Cor 12:12), where he concentrates on the roles and responsibilities of the members of the body. Here he emphasizes the preeminence of Christ as head of the body, which is the church.

The image of body illustrates two ecojustice principles: interconnectedness and purpose. Interconnectedness underscores the mutual dependence the various parts of the body have on one another. Purpose emphasizes the dynamic design to which each of the diverse parts of the body contributes in its own way.

Paul has acclaimed the preeminence of Christ: "He is the beginning" (Col 2:18; cf. Prov 8:22), the "firstborn." For the second time in this hymn Paul identifies Christ as the "firstborn." Here he does not use the term in its cosmological sense, as he did earlier in the hymn, but as a way of explaining his soteriology, or theology of salvation. "Firstborn from the dead" refers to the primacy of Christ's resurrection, his having been born to the new life of eschatological fulfillment. As "firstborn from the dead" Christ demonstrates his supremacy over all other members of the church and, at the same time, guarantees their future resurrection. Having already established Christ as the firstborn of all creation, Paul moves easily to presenting him as firstborn of the new creation. Here we see that protology (first things) is fulfilled in eschatology (last things). Paul argues that Christ's resurrection confirms his supremacy over all creation. In this way Christ enjoys the first place in all things.

Throughout the poem Christ has been portrayed as the agent of God, the image that represents and functions for God within all of creation. Paul does not rest with this description. There is yet another aspect of Christ's preeminence that he wishes to emphasize. He further maintains that "in him all the fullness of God was pleased to dwell" (Col 1:19). While this statement might sound like an assertion of Christ's divinity, it is probably better to understand it here in line with the focus of the entire hymn, which is interested more in how Christ functions than in any divine essence or reality he might claim. Thus, the phrase "in him all the fullness of God was pleased to dwell" maintains that Christ's representation/function in God's stead is not limited as the representation/function of the man and woman as image of

God was limited. Nor is it shared by any of the astral deities, as the false teachers seem to be telling the Colossians. This fullness of God belongs totally and uniquely to Christ.

Paul's introduction of the concept of reconciliation indicates that the unity and harmony of the world have somehow been ruptured. He is not interested here in the cause of this rupture but rather its extent and the manner in which it will be repaired (Col 1:20). The reconciliation of which he speaks is not merely appeasement among human beings or between human beings and God. Since the entire scope of this christological hymn is cosmic, the reconciliation of which Paul speaks is between God and all elements of the cosmos, "whether on earth or in heaven" (Col 1:20). Many of the religious cults of the day taught that a breach in the relationship with a deity required some ritual enactment to reconcile this estrangement. This frequently included a sacrifice. Paul only alludes to the concept of sacrifice, maintaining that it is the blood of Christ, and not that of an animal offered in appeasement, that accomplishes this reconciliation.

It is important to note that the death of Jesus, the event that effected this reconciliation, took place in history, not in some spiritual realm outside of or beyond the world of flesh and blood, as some of the astral cults claimed. When Paul speaks of the blood of the cross he is referring to the entire mystery of salvation, namely, the death of Jesus brought to fulfillment in his resurrection. He argues that Christ shows that he and only he can bring all things to their final fulfillment, contrary to the claims of the false teachers. According to Paul, the entire universe was brought into existence through Christ, has been sustained by him, and has been reconciled to God through his death and resurrection.

Paul's concept of a cosmic Christ may be very foreign to the contemporary reader. However, it must be remembered that Paul was addressing major issues facing the people of his time, not ours. Practical theologian that he was, he spoke out of the worldview and employed the very concepts of the teachings he was challenging. People today possess a very different understanding of the cosmos and would probably not speak about Christ's influence in the same way. Still, many of the underlying concepts Paul employed in his arguments resonate with contemporary theology.

Paul has articulated a cosmology that is christocentric, not anthropocentric. In his thinking, the value of the components of the universe—"all things in heaven and on earth . . . things visible and invisible" (Col 1:16)—is not determined by their usefulness to human beings but by their having been created through the agency of Christ, who holds all things together. Nothing is excluded here; nothing lacks importance or worth. The repetition of the phrase "all things" makes this quite clear. This very rich poem depicts Christ, image of God and firstborn of all creation, as embracing the entire community of Earth, reconciling all of creation to God. This is a glorious picture.

In Christ

Ephesus was a large seaport on the western coast of Asia Minor in what is today modern Turkey. It was, in fact, the first and probably the most prominent metropolis of the Roman province of Asia. While scholars agree that Paul spent time there (Acts 20:31), the majority of them do not believe that he wrote this letter. It lacks the familiarity found in many of the authentic Pauline letters, a familiarity that would have been obvious had he resided in the city for any amount of time. Furthermore, the message of the letter is more a summary of the major elements of Paul's teaching than it is an address to specific issues facing the Christians in that city. The exact genre of this writing also raises questions about authorship and date of origin. While it lacks the features of an epistle or a letter, some scholars maintain that it is a circular letter sent to various communities as a summary of current Christian teaching. Others classify it as a theological discourse or a homily. Its similarity to, even dependence upon, the Letter to the Colossians has led scholars to date its writing ca. 80–90 CE, written somewhere in Asia Minor by a second-generation Pauline Christian.

The Letter to the Ephesians, even more than the Letter to the Colossians, presents a picture of a cosmic Christ. However, features of this picture are spread throughout the letter rather than contained and developed within a discrete passage, as is found in Colossians (Col 1:15–20). Two passages in particular sketch the general outlines of this cosmic Christology. Both are found in the first chapter. The first is a prayer of blessing. Two sections in this prayer are pertinent to this study:

> Blessed be the God and Father of our Lord Jesus Christ, who has blessed us in Christ with every spiritual blessing in the heavenly places, just as he chose us in Christ before the foundation of the world to be holy and blameless before him in love. (Eph 1:3–4)

Features of this prayer resemble the Jewish prayer of blessing known as the *berakah*, in which God is praised for the blessings of creation and redemption. Here the themes of creation and redemption overlap. While the main focus is election, two phrases provide a glimpse into Paul's[11] cosmological context within which this election takes place: "heavenly places" and "foundation of the world."

The Greek word translated "heavenly places" is rare, found in only four other places in the New Testament, all of them in the Letter to the Ephesians:

> God . . . seated him at his right hand in the heavenly places. (1:20)

> seated us with him in the heavenly places (2:6)

> made known to the rulers and authorities in the heavenly places (3:10)

> against the spiritual forces of evil in the heavenly places (6:12)

Together these references suggest that the heavenly realms were inhabited by God, Christ, those joined to Christ, and some spiritual forces of evil. Such a view corresponds to the cosmology of the time, which maintained that there were various dimensions

---

[11] The traditional practice of referring to the author of this pseudonymous letter as Paul is followed here.

or spheres of the heavens[12] and that these celestial realms held both good and evil forces.[13] Reinterpreting this commonly held notion of the cosmos to fit his Christology, Paul states that, following his resurrection, Christ is now seated in the heavenly realms at God's right hand, the recognized place of honor (Eph 1:20). Those joined to Christ are seated with him in the "heavenly realms" (1:20; 2:6), and there they are blessed with "every spiritual blessing" (1:3). Such exaltation and honor suggest that the spiritual forces of evil also found in the "heavenly places" (6:12) have been defeated. All of this has been accomplished by the power of God. In Jewish apocalyptic thinking this defeat signifies the dawning of the eschatological age of fulfillment.

Despite the defeat of the forces of evil, the cosmic battle is not yet over. Paul tells his readers that our struggle is against "the spiritual forces of evil in the heavenly places" (Eph 6:12). This is probably a reference to what Colossians calls "thrones or dominions or rulers or powers" (Col 1:16), the elemental spirits that gnostic philosophy claimed controlled the universe. Followers of that worldview performed various ascetical practices meant to release them from their spiritual imprisonment in their bodies. Paul rejects this disdain for the body, arguing that the struggle is not "against blood and flesh" (Eph 6:12).[14] Though these elemental spirits have been conquered by God through Christ, human beings must still struggle with their influence in the world. Once again we see the Christian eschatological paradox of the already-but-not-yet.

"Foundation of the world" *(kósmos)* is a second cosmological phrase found in this passage that speaks of what has come to be known as the doctrine of election. Contrary to what many think, this doctrine does not merely refer to predestined salvation but, in accord with the Jewish understanding of election, it denotes

---

[12] Seven seems to have been the most popular number of heavenly spheres, with God living in the "highest heaven" (Matt 21:9; Mark 11:10; Luke 19:38).

[13] This could explain why those who ascended into heaven were often accompanied by angelic guardians.

[14] The Greek simply has "blood and flesh," not "enemies of blood and flesh," as some translations suggest.

a call to responsibility, as we read in God's blessing to Abram: "In you all the families of the earth shall be blessed" (Gen 12:3). Paul insists that the union of the believers with Christ was part of God's plan even before the foundation of the cosmos. Here is an example of the overlap of the themes of creation and redemption. God's plan may have preceded actual creation, but its unfolding takes place within the world of human beings, not in some ethereal world of spirits.

A second passage in this prayer underscores the revelation of God's plan:

> With all wisdom and insight he has made known to us the mystery of his will, according to his good pleasure that he set forth in Christ, as a plan for the fullness of time, to gather up all things in him, things in heaven and things on earth. (Eph 1:8–10)

Paul uses language from mystery religions current at the time, though he reinterprets the concepts that they convey. Mysteries were thought to be secrets known only to the members of the respective sect. Paul states that the mystery of God's will, which had been "hidden for ages" (3:9), "was made known to me" (3:3), and through his preaching is made known to all. There is no secrecy here; no one can boast of privileged knowledge. The mystery is the divine plan that all things, both in heaven and on earth, will be gathered together in Christ. Though this plan has *already* taken shape and been revealed, it has *not yet* been fully realized. "Fullness of time" *(kairós)* points to the future age of realization. The verb translated "gather up" (Eph 1:10) really means "to gather again under one head." This verb suggests that a rupture has occurred in what was originally harmonious. Similar to the reference to reconciliation in Colossians (1:20), the tradition of enmity found in Genesis 3 lies behind this idea. The cosmic inclusiveness of this gathering reflects what is also stated in Colossians (1:15–20). In Ephesians, as in that earlier letter, the cosmic Christ draws all creation to himself.

Ephesians places less emphasis on future fulfillment than does Colossians. Perhaps this is because the Christians at the time of the writing of the Letter to the Ephesians were not looking forward to an imminent return of Christ as the Colossians seem to have been. The Letter to the Ephesians concentrates on the present as the time of fulfillment and, thus, exhorts believers to give living proof of eschatological fulfillment through the character of their lives. This focus on realized eschatology leads us to the final verses of this chapter, wherein is found another sketch of the cosmic Christ:

> And he has put all things under his feet and has made him the head over all things for the church, which is his body, the fullness of him who fills all in all. (Eph 1:22–23)

Many commentators considered these verses an early Christian credal statement. In it, Christ is depicted as a conqueror. This image calls to mind many ancient portrayals of victorious rulers seated on thrones with a foot on the neck of an enemy. This same scene is sketched in Psalm 110: "I make your enemies your footstool." Many today find this image troubling. They see it as oppressive, suggesting the conquest of the natural world. However, this depiction is not an example of brutal domination, of the strong overpowering the weak. Both the passage from Ephesians and the one from Psalm 110 suggest a struggle between good and evil, with good emerging triumphant. In the Letter to the Ephesians the opponents are the elemental spirits of gnostic philosophy referred to as the rulers, the authorities, and the powers (1:21). The peace that follows victory is often exemplified through scenes of natural tranquility. However, the victory that won the peace is not as easily portrayed. Here it is an image of the conquering ruler.

Christ is next acknowledged as head over all things, made so by God. Earlier in this chapter the phrase "all things" was understood to include "things in heaven and things on earth" (Eph 1:10). In other words, Christ is head over the entire cosmos. Paul then makes an extraordinary statement. He claims that God made Christ the head of the cosmos for the sake of the church. "In Christ we have also obtained an inheritance . . . so that we, who were the first to set our hope on Christ, might live for the praise of his glory" (1:11–12). Here the cosmological theme gives precedence to an ecclesiological one, which continues to the end of verse 14. This does not imply that cosmology itself is secondary to ecclesiology, for this first chapter begins and ends with the image of the cosmic Christ. It is instead a shift in focus in order to emphasize the importance of the church in the eternal plan of God. Once again we see Paul employing the imagery and arguments of his day to countermand the claims of his opponents.

Several themes in these passages from Ephesians resonate with various ecojustice principles. First, the idea of a divine plan resembles the principle of purpose, which states that the universe, Earth, and all the members of the community of Earth are part of a dynamic cosmic design. The difference between this principle and the passage in Ephesians lies in the character of the design. The ecoprinciple presumes a material or corporeal universe, while Ephesians includes both material and spiritual realities. Furthermore, the cosmic unity that is the focus of the ecoprinciple is held together by the natural laws to which all elements of the universe are subject, while Christ is the cause and goal of the unity spoken of in Ephesians. Radical ecologists might see the significance of the cosmic Christ as a form of theological anthropocentrism. However, while the resurrection of Jesus as the Christ is pivotal in this theological perspective, it is not the humanity of Jesus that holds all things together but divine power working through Christ. As Christ gathers both spiritual and material realities together, the uniqueness of every component is recognized and valued. Each is now free to function according to its respective nature, thus contributing to the overall goal of the divine plan.

Eschatological Fulfillment

The overarching message of Paul's teaching is the good news that eschatological fulfillment has been accomplished through the resurrection of Christ. In teaching this Paul did not merely repeat what he had learned from others. He reinterpreted earlier tradition, creating something new while retaining the fundamental meaning of the original religious message. In other words, earlier traditions were retrieved but had to be reinterpreted if they were to continue to be revelatory for a new generation of believers. All of Paul's theology, whether it is explicitly stated in cosmological language or not, flows from his understanding of this fulfillment. His Christology depicts Christ as realizing God's plan; his ethics challenges believers to live as if they have been saved, for they have indeed been saved; his ecclesiology sketches the church as an assembly of those enjoying the fruits of the divine promises. However, while fulfillment had indeed been accomplished in Christ, it was still unfolding. Hence, the concept of already-but-not-yet. To use contemporary cosmological language, eschatological fulfillment is an emerging reality. Paul's message was clearly good news for believers of his day. The challenge of every age of believers is the furthering of this message, its articulation in the language and concepts of the prevailing cosmology.

Most of the ecojustice principles correspond to Paul's cosmological Christology and eschatology.

1. Paul recognized the intrinsic value of all creation, for he claims that all things in heaven and on earth, things visible and invisible, were created in and for Christ.
2. The oneness of which Paul consistently speaks corresponds with the notion of interconnectedness.
3. Creation has voice, and it groans in birthpangs as it awaits its transformation.
4. God's plan, which will be brought to fulfillment in the fullness of time, corresponds to the idea of a dynamic cosmic design.
5. While the principle of mutual custodianship focuses on physical reality, the union of all reality in and through Christ, both heaven and earth, both the visible and the invisible, suggests an even more comprehensive harmony than does the principle.
6. There is no need for creation to offer any resistance to injustice, because through Christ, all things have been reconciled with God.

Despite the fact that Paul's cosmology was very different than the view that is prevalent today, the passages examined in this chapter continue to be retrieved and reinterpreted. Insights from contemporary cosmology prompt us to ask new questions. For example:

1. Standing on the threshold of a new appreciation of the community of Earth, how do we understand the character of our created world?
2. Now that science has demonstrated that there are really millions of universes, what is the scope of Christ's supremacy beyond the dimensions of our own universe?

Questions such as these leave us standing in awe of the mysteries of God's love of creation, mysteries of which we are a part but that we cannot even begin to fathom.

> "A new heaven and a new earth"
>
> —Revelation 21:1

Chapter Seven

The last book of the Bible, Revelation, is probably the most difficult one to understand. It tells of monsters with many heads and horns; cosmic disasters such as falling stars and the moon losing its light; and upheaval on Earth through plagues, fires, and the destruction of life forms. It also describes celestial wonders such as heavenly choirs and magnificent liturgies, the end of suffering and death, and entrance into an experience of wondrous transformation. This is both a frightening and a consoling book. However, much depends on how it is understood.

Readers today are familiar with what has come to be known as high fantasy literature. Examples include J. R. R. Tolkien's *The Lord of the Rings*, C. S. Lewis's *The Chronicles of Narnia*, and J. K. Rowling's *Harry Potter* series. While such stories thrill the childlike and naive, more mature readers know that these are really a form of the morality chronicle, a narrative whose details may not all be historically accurate but that teaches a profound truth. Though very different from one another, the narratives mentioned above have several features in common. First and foremost, they all describe the struggle between the forces of good and the forces of evil, with good triumphing in the end. However, this triumph does not occur without characters within the story having to face and overcome great challenges. Such stories never cease to be popular because they have captured one of the universal characteristics of every human life, namely, the need to come to grips with the difficulties that life inevitably includes and to be better for the struggle.

The biblical Book of Revelation has much in common with such literature. This is not to say that it is fantasy literature meant to entertain the naive. Rather, it is to point out that stories told with extraordinary, even bizarre, symbolism are not foreign to today's readers. However, these readers may not expect to find such symbolic accounts in the Bible, or they are not familiar with the profound religious meaning behind the biblical symbolism. This is probably because the symbolism, which belongs to a very different culture, is foreign to us today. However, if we understand the meaning of these symbols, we realize that underneath them is a story of the struggle between the forces of good and the forces of evil, with good triumphing in the end. We also see and appreciate the awesomeness and graciousness of God in this triumph, a feature that is at the heart of the Book of Revelation, though not found explicitly in the high fantasy literature mentioned above.

The very first word in this biblical book is *apokálypsis* (revelation), a word that identifies both the book's literary form and its style of writing. This type of book was relatively common in the ancient world. Though no actual apocalypse is found in the Old Testament, several prophetic books contain sections that are profoundly apocalyptic (Isa 24—27; Zech 12—14; Joel 3). Furthermore, a number of non-biblical Jewish apocalypses appeared during the Greco-Roman period, the time when Revelation is thought to have been written.

The standard form of such writing is a narrative in which the secrets of the origin and destiny of the cosmos are revealed to a chosen person by an otherworldly being, usually an angel. Some of these writings describe supernatural journeys in which the working of the cosmos—the sun, the moon, the stars, the weather, the establishment of the calendar, and so on—are revealed to a seer. Others trace the major events of history (past and present) leading to a cosmic crisis in which the powers of evil are vanquished and total transformation takes place. The revelation itself might occur in a dream, a vision, a trance, or an auditory experience.

The secret character of the revelation is retained by means of symbolic imagery that functions as a kind of code language. However, much of this imagery was somewhat standard in the ancient world, originating from Ancient Near Eastern mythology.

For example, wild beasts frequently represent world powers; certain numbers have symbolic meaning (for example, 4 signifies fullness; 7 is a sign of perfection); colors stand for various characteristics (for example, white denotes victory; purple signifies royalty). The secret character of apocalypses notwithstanding, the purpose of this kind of writing is revelation, not concealment. In other words, an apocalypse seeks to reveal mysteries that have been concealed until now. Finally, those who author an apocalypse usually claim the identity and authority of a great person from the past, thus bestowing extraordinary importance to it. Such pseudonymity also contributes to difficulty in dating the writing.

Literary Context

There is no question about the apocalyptic character of the Book of Revelation. However, there is quite a bit of discussion regarding the fundamental literary form of the book. Is it a genuine apocalypse? Might it instead be a form of prophecy? Or is it a letter? The use of metaphoric language and symbols as well as the inclusion of visions and their interpretation certainly correspond to the style of the apocalypse. However, the events described do not hark back to an earlier age as they would in a true apocalypse; rather, these events pertain to the time of those for whom the message of the book was intended. In line with this, the revelation provides an explanation of current events, not long-concealed cosmic secrets as found in a true apocalypse. Finally, the author of this book is identified. Such considerations lead one to question whether this is an authentic apocalypse.

Revelation itself identifies its content as prophecy (Rev 1:3). Many interpreters maintain that apocalyptic thinking and writing originated out of and is an extension of prophecy. Like prophecy, Revelation provides profound insight into the time of the seer. It warns those guilty of transgression what punishment their behavior deserves, and it promises relief to the innocent who are suffering. However, the struggle between good and evil that it describes is not merely historical, dealing with social or political matters as is the case with prophecy. Instead, the struggle is cosmic, including all dimensions of heaven and of Earth.

While the first verses designate the book as an apocalypse (Rev 1:1) and then as a prophecy (1:3), they are introductory and written in the third person. Beginning with verse 4 the book manifests the features of a letter. It identifies the sender (John), the addressees (the seven churches that are in Asia), and the greeting ("Grace to you and peace"). It continues this epistolary character throughout the rest of the book. Despite these features, chapter 4 begins with reports of visions that are definitely apocalyptic in nature. These diverse characteristics have led most contemporary scholars to identify Revelation as a hybrid document, a visionary apocalyptic writing, expressed in the form of an epistle that functions prophetically. Put another way, Revelation is an apocalyptic-prophetic letter.

Though the seer in Revelation is identified as John (Rev 1:1, 4, 9; 22:8), the specific identity of this John has been debated over the years. Initially, he was presumed to be the son of Zebedee, the disciple of Jesus, the same John who authored the Gospel and the Letters that bear his name. Differences in the style of writing, the character of the Greek in which these books were written, and their differing theological concerns have led most contemporary scholars to conclude that the Gospel of John and Revelation had different authors. As for the Letters, they were probably written much later than the Gospel by someone from within the Johannine community. Today, most hold that Revelation was written by a Jewish-Christian prophet named John who was neither the apostle nor the author of other writings attributed to John.

Scholars agree that the book was written sometime between 92 and 96 CE, during the reign of the Roman Emperor Domitian. They are not in agreement as to whether the struggle described in the book refers to a persecution launched by that emperor, since there is no extra-biblical evidence of such a persecution at this time. The disasters described in the book may be meant to be emblematic of any or all struggles that would face the early church.

Perhaps the most disputed aspect of Revelation is the method employed in interpreting the book. Most likely the original audience understood the meaning and significance of its symbolism, and so interpreting its message did not present the problem for them. However, this may not have been the case when the book was read by later generations who were unfamiliar with the references behind the symbols. As a result, over the years people developed various ways of interpretation. One approach is a non-historical method of reading the book, one that is unconcerned with any historical references and is interested only in timeless truths. This approach understands the conflict depicted in the book as the ever-present struggle between good and evil. A strength of this approach is its ongoing relevance, for reading in this way can give religious meaning to the struggle of every age, and it can also offer every age the hope of final victory. On the other hand, this approach bypasses the question of the inspiration granted the original author and the revelatory value of meaning derived at any previous period of history.

Another approach traces the history of the church through the ages, interpreting Revelation as predictive prophecy. This approach understands the time of the interpreter as the end of the age, thus granting the book immediate relevance. However, this would mean that it had little or no significance for the original audience or any audience other than that of the present interpreter. This approach also misunderstands prophecy as concern for the future rather than insight into the present. A similar approach claims that Revelation is exclusively concerned with the end of the age. In this view the interpreter stands on the threshold of the end of time, maintaining that the events symbolically portrayed in the book are unfolding in current social and political events. This method of interpretation has become quite popular among many contemporary evangelicals. This approach denies the book's relevance at any time in history other than the present, and it misunderstands the focus of biblical prophecy as predictive.

The last and most common method of interpretation today employs the same critical methods of interpretation for understanding this book as it does for any other biblical book. This means that the intent of the original author is honored, while the ongoing inspiration of the Spirit continues to open the passage to meanings. The challenge in this approach resides in the move from the way the original community would have understood the meaning of the symbolism to the insights into it gained by a contemporary community. As with all contemporary biblical interpretation the meaning gleaned from a careful analysis of the passage is refashioned or restated so that it is meaningful to a new audience.

The final matter under the heading of literary context is the placement of Revelation in the entire collection of biblical books. First, the inclusion of this book in the list of books referred to as sacred scripture did not happen without struggle. From the very beginning the nature of the book, its symbolic grotesqueness, and its apocalyptic violence have troubled many believers. However, its positive, even glorious conclusion brings to fulfillment many theological questions such as the justice of God, the role played by Christ in the creation of the cosmos, and the gathering of all believers in the embrace of God.

Revelation also brings the entire biblical story to conclusion. Genesis opens that story with the account of the creation of heaven and Earth, while Revelation announces the new heaven and the new Earth. The mythic features of Eden are held in balance with the symbolic features of the new Jerusalem. The original time and the final time imply a theological correspondence between the beginning and the end. Revelation's placement in the Bible suggests that it brings the biblical story of creation/salvation to conclusion.

"Then I saw"

One of the features of Revelation is a series of visions that depicts various natural disasters. This theme runs throughout major sections of the book like a fugue, sometimes playing clearly yet without force and at others time presenting itself with increasing intensity. In an opening vision John beholds the glory of God (Rev 4:1–11) and the Lamb that had been slain but was now "worthy . . . to receive power and riches, wisdom and strength, honor and power, and blessing" (5:12). It is the Lamb who opens the seven seals of the scroll that contains the secrets of the cosmos, an explicit apocalyptic aspect of this biblical book. As each seal is opened, a form of affliction is unleashed on Earth through the agency of a horseman.

The colors of the horses on which these horsemen ride symbolize various plagues. The first horse is white (Rev 6:1–2), the color of victory, a victory achieved through aggression and conquest. This horse signifies human lust for war. The second horse is blood red (6:3–4), representing the violence that human beings perpetrate against one another. Scales are carried by the horseman on the third steed (6:5–6), the black one. This suggests that, because war destroys crops and causes famine, the fruits of Earth are scarce and must be meted out. The rider on the fourth and final horse epitomizes death. Its pale green color is the color of a corpse (6:7–8). Some commentators see a natural progression of affliction in the order in which these horsemen appear. First is aggression; aggression results in war and bloodshed; war then brings on famine and starvation; and finally, all of these afflictions lead to death. Though these sufferings are directed toward human beings, the other members of the community of Earth also suffer the consequences of human violence. With the fifth seal the sufferings unfolding on Earth are replaced by the conferral of a white robe of victory on those who have remained faithful despite having been forced to forfeit their lives for their fidelity. Although they receive the white robe, their final reward will have to wait for the short interlude between the opening of the sixth and seventh seals.

Cosmic disasters characteristic of the apocalyptic tradition tumble out as the sixth seal is opened. These include earthquakes, the darkening of the sun, the moon turning red as blood, and stars falling from the sky (Rev 6:12–13a). Such occurrences were considered portents of the long-anticipated and now approaching day of the Lord. This day was initially thought to be a day of judgment (Amos 5:20). After the exile it was considered the future time of the final struggle between good and evil, the eschatological moment of transition from the present age of sinfulness to the age of fulfillment. The apocalyptic disasters associated with this momentous day symbolize the rupture that takes place as one age ends and the next is born. As we have seen above, this rupture came to be known as the "birthpangs of the Messiah."

One might expect that with the opening of the seventh seal the secrets contained within the scroll would be revealed. However, this does not happen. Instead, there is silence in heaven for half an hour, and then seven angels appear, each with a trumpet. The eschatological judgment predicted in a general way in the account of the seals is now described with more detail in this vision of seven angels (Rev 8:1—11:19). The trumpets act as warnings of impending disaster. Just as the seals unleashed heavenly cataclysms, so the trumpets alert the seer to earthly adversity. The seventh trumpet announces the arrival of the reign of the Messiah (11:15–19).

Pertinent to this study is the nature of the disasters announced by these trumpets. Five of the disasters call to mind several of the plagues endured at the time of the Exodus from Egypt (Exod 7—9). Though they do not conform exactly to the plagues in content or order of occurrence, the similarities are striking:[1]

1st trumpet	Rev 8:7	hail, fire, blood	7th plague	Exod 9:22–25
2nd trumpet	Rev 8:8–9	sea into blood	1st plague	Exod 7:20–24
3rd trumpet	Rev 8:10–11	bitter water	1st plague	Exod 7:20–24
4th trumpet	Rev 8:12	darkness	9th plague	Exod 10:21–23
5th trumpet	Rev 9:1–11	locusts	8th plague	Exod 10:12–20

A similar catastrophe is recorded in Joel:

> I will show portents in the heavens and on the earth, blood and fire and columns of smoke. The sun shall be turned to darkness, and the moon to blood, before the great and terrible day of the LORD comes. (Joel 2:30–31)

In this prophetic book, the cosmic upheavals are clearly portents signaling the impending day of the Lord. This day has been understood in various ways down through the centuries. As the above passage indicates, the prophet Joel thought it would be a day of judgment for sinfulness. Much later, Paul looked forward to it as the day when Christ would return:

> For you yourselves know very well that the day of the Lord will come like a thief in the night. (1 Thess 5:2)

The author of Revelation considers it the day that will usher in the reign of God. The cosmic trauma described here includes the destruction of Earth and the vegetation it produces, the destruction of the sea and living things within it, and the darkening of celestial bodies, all of which can be considered aspects of the

---

[1] See Wilfrid J. Harrington, OP, *Revelation*, Sacra Pagina 16 (Collegeville, MN: Liturgical Press, 1993), 107.

eschatological transition from this age to the age of fulfillment, not merely the punishing wrath of an avenging God. The three interpretations given for the day of the Lord do not conflict with one another. They simply emphasize one aspect over the others: judgment, dawning of the age of fulfillment, or the return of Christ.

As indicated earlier, the plagues of Egypt and those described in Revelation function in very different ways. The Exodus tradition recounts contests between the arrogantly presumed divine power of Egypt's pharaoh and the proclaimed and proven power of the God of Israel. Not only did God demonstrate unquestioned control over the forces of nature when Egypt's magicians could not, but God accomplished these feats within the land of Egypt itself, the land thought to be under the jurisdiction of Pharaoh.[2] In Joel, the account of the locusts probably originated from the experience of an actual plague (Joel 1:1–20). The prophet then used this experience as a metaphor first for an invading army (2:1–17) and then as an apocalyptic image announcing the day of the Lord (1:15; 2:1–2, 11, 31; 32:14). While the symbolism found in Revelation can be interpreted in various ways, both the cosmic upheaval and unbelievable human suffering foreshadow the great day of the Lord and, therefore, can be seen as a dimension of the "birthpangs of the Messiah."

As in a fugue, reports of victory and celebration are followed by yet a third series of revelations. The first series was seals; the second was trumpets; the third is bowls. In this final series all of the visions include some form of cosmic upheaval. The contents of the first bowl causes sores on those who have committed themselves to evil (Rev 16:2). The contents of the second bowl turns the sea to blood, killing all living things within it (16:3). When the third bowl is emptied, rivers and springs turn to blood (16:4). When the fourth bowl is turned over, the sun scorches those who are unfaithful (16:8). The throne of the evil one is cast into darkness by the contents of the fifth bowl (16:10–11). The waters of the Euphrates are dried up by the substance in the

---

[2] A later version of the Egyptian plagues is found in the Wisdom of Solomon. There, God's power over nature is interpreted as a sign of the superiority of the faith and religious tradition of the Jewish people over the philosophical tradition of the Greeks (Wis 11:2—19:22).

sixth bowl (16:12). Finally, the seventh bowl is emptied into the air, causing lightning, thunder, and earthquakes (16:17–18). Thus Earth, air, and water are all affected in this series of disasters.

Once again, elements of the account of the plagues as found in the Exodus tradition lie behind this vision. The sores caused by the first bowl call to mind the sores suffered by the Egyptian people in the sixth plague (Exod 9:8–11); waters turning to blood is reminiscent of the third plague (Exod 7:20–21). The plagues resulting from the overturned bowls share another characteristic with the Exodus tradition, a characteristic not found in the visions of the seals or those of the trumpets. Neither the pharaoh in the earlier tradition nor the people depicted here in Revelation learn from the afflictions they are forced to endure; they do not repent of their sinfulness.

The visions of destruction end with an authoritative declaration of finality:

> A loud voice came out of the temple, from the throne, saying, "It is done!" And there came flashes of lightning, rumblings, peals of thunder, and a violent earthquake, such as had not occurred since people were upon the earth, so violent was that earthquake. (Rev 16:17–18)

This is not just any voice. It is a voice from the throne. The lightning, thunder, and quaking of Earth are signs of cosmic upheaval as well as of divine theophany or manifestation. Given the character of these visions, they could well signify both. They primarily announce the final destruction of evil, which is further described in the chapters that follow. However, it is divine justice that majestically reveals itself in these cosmic occurrences. The voice from the temple announces that the upheavals are done; the purification of the cosmos resulting from those upheavals is done; the birthpangs are done! Something new is born.

As with all of the biblical writing, the message of Revelation had immediate relevance. The eschatological significance intended by the author was not merely an exercise in creative writing. It bore social and political meaning. The letters to the seven churches found at the beginning of the book provide hints of some of the struggles facing those churches. The plagues and other disasters depicted in the chapters that follow are meant for people within those churches. The beasts that are portrayed as having been defeated represent the social and political enemies of the upright. As already stated, those for whom this book was originally intended would have understood the symbolism and appreciated the warnings described.

Regardless of the method one uses to interpret the calamities so vividly described in Revelation, the author's purpose in presenting them in this way is clear. They are warnings, meant to encourage the fainthearted to remain steadfast lest they suffer such catastrophes and to exhort the erring to change their ways. The power and majesty of the message of Revelation notwithstanding, the question raised in this study remains: Is all of this accomplished at the expense of Earth and the other members of the community of Earth? A close look at the vision of eschatological fulfillment will put these visions of apocalyptic disaster in proper perspective.

"A new heaven and a new earth"

Then I saw a new heaven and a new earth; for the first heaven and the first earth had passed away, and the sea was no more. And I saw the holy city, the new Jerusalem, coming down out of heaven from God, prepared as a bride adorned for her husband. . . . And I heard a loud voice from the throne saying, "See, the home of God is among mortals." And the one who was seated on the throne said, "See, I am making all things new." (Rev 21:1–3a, 5)

The report of this last revelatory experience contains imagery that is quite traditional, though it is reshaped in ways that are extraordinary. The phrase "new heavens and a new earth" is found in an oracle of salvation in the third part of the Book of Isaiah:

For I am about to create new heavens and a new earth; the former things shall not be remembered or come to mind. (Isa 65:17)

This passage probably reflects a time after the Israelites had returned from exile in Babylon. Though no longer enslaved, they were still dissatisfied with their social and political circumstances, and so they looked to the future. Found in an apocalyptic section at the end of the Book of Isaiah, this section promises the people future peace and prosperity.[3] This promise was cherished and preserved by the people of ancient Israel down through the centuries, thus enabling the writer of Revelation to appropriate it and interpret it through the lens of faith in Christ, who was seen as the fulfillment of all eschatological promises.

The passage in Revelation raises some fundamental questions for those concerned about issues of ecojustice, particularly the principle of intrinsic value. Are this new heaven and new Earth fundamentally different from the old heaven and old Earth? If so, does this mean that Revelation and the entire apocalyptic eschatological tradition are anti-Earth, or anti–natural world? If they are not different, in what way are they new? And if new, what is the relationship between the old and the new? A look at the meaning of Greek words will help to answer these questions.

The Greek language has two words for new: *néos*, which denotes something that is new in time; and *kainós*, which means new in character. New Testament writers usually chose *kainós* when referring to anything related to eschatological fulfillment. This is the word found in the above passage from Revelation. The use of *kainós* suggests that the new heaven and the new Earth are not merely newer versions of the past but possess some kind of different character. If this is the case, does this newness mean that they are totally distinct from the past? The Greek word can certainly mean this, but it does not have that sense here. When trying to describe the radical newness that broke into the world through the life, death, and resurrection of Jesus, the New Testament writers employed language and imagery known to their readers, but they opened the meaning of that language and imagery in creative ways. Most likely, such is the case here. In other words, though totally new, the new heaven and new Earth are not separated from what was. This conclu-

---

[3] "New heaven and new earth" is found in other apocalyptic writings, such as 1 Enoch 45:4–5.

sion is based on arguments found in Paul's teaching about the resurrected body.

In his First Letter to the Corinthians, Paul discusses the kind of body possessed by those who died united to Christ:

> But someone will ask, "How are the dead raised? With what kind of body do they come?" (1 Cor 15:35)

He uses an agricultural metaphor to describe both the fundamental connection between the body before death and the body after death, and the radical newness that emerges out of the old:

> So it is with the resurrection of the dead. What is sown is perishable, what is raised is imperishable. It is sown in dishonor, it is raised in glory. It is sown in weakness, it is raised in power. It is sown a physical body, it is raised a spiritual body. (1 Cor 15:42–44a)

The connection that Paul makes is quite clear. There is indeed something radically new in the bodies of those raised from the dead. However, this newness is somehow dependent on what previously existed. For example, there would be no blossom or fruit if there would have been no seed. True, something of the seed decays and is even destroyed. But something of its essence remains. So it is with the new heaven and new Earth. There is something radically new, but it emerges from the old. It is clear that neither Paul nor the writer of Revelation disdain what is earthly. They do not believe that eschatological fulfillment means that what is of Earth is cast aside or destroyed. Rather, like the physical body of Jesus and the bodies of those united to him in faith, all is transformed into eschatological newness. It is not so much that new things are made, but that all things are made new in a new sense.

This idea of new creation is found in another passage from Paul, this time in the Second Letter to the Corinthians:

> So if anyone is in Christ, there is a new [kainós] creation: everything old has passed away; see, everything has become new [kainós]! (2 Cor 5:17)

It is clear from this passage that Paul believes that this newness is not determined by temporal standards or concepts. What is new is not simply a replacement. Rather, it enjoys a new state of transformed human existence.

An essential characteristic of this newness is the triumph over evil and death and the end of suffering, all aspects of human existence before its eschatological transformation. This triumph is referred to by the statement in Revelation that

> the sea is no more. (Rev 21:1b)

This expression calls to mind the ancient Mesopotamian characterization of the sea as unruly waters. The image probably originated from the people's experience of the unpredictable and treacherous overflow of the waters of the Tigris and the Euphrates. In many of the creation myths of that area, the evil god is called Yam, a word which in Hebrew is translated sea. This sea appears in many poetic sections of the Bible, and in each instance the sea is under the control of the God of Israel.

Isaiah praises the creator who in a cosmic battle conquered the sea:

> He has stretched out his hand over the sea,
> he has shaken the kingdoms. (Isa 23:11)

The Psalmist also lauds God's creative power:

> He gathered the waters of the sea as in a
>   bottle;
> he put the deeps in storehouses. (Ps 33:7)

In the challenges that lead Job to realize his human limitations, God poses the question:

> Who shut in the sea with doors when it burst out from the
> womb? (Job 38:8)

Such passages show that these cosmic waters are no equal to the powers of the mighty God. In Revelation's vision of eschatological fulfillment, the author announces that the threat posed from the very beginning by the forces of evil has been definitively defeated: "the sea is no more."

The passage from Revelation includes a description of the new *(kainós)* Jerusalem coming down from heaven as a bride. Many gnostic religions maintain that perfection entails transcending what is of Earth and rising to a new and esoteric spiritual manner of existence, often thought to be a form of rapture into heaven. The scene here is very different. There is no rising above Earth. Rather, there is descending to Earth: the heavenly city comes down, and heaven and Earth seem to merge. Remarkably, this merging takes place in the realm of the human:[4]

"See, the home of God is among mortals." (Rev 21:3a)

Contrary to any gnostic anti-body or anti-Earth perspective, Revelation offers the reader an anti-dualistic vision of eschatological communion. Resurrection is not a mystical, out-of-body experience. It is a total bodily transformation. Those of us who still live a physical life have no idea what this newness might be like, nor do we know where or how this transformation might take place. Nonetheless, it is a promise that is found in both testaments, woven throughout the entire Bible. At times it is indistinct, even shrouded in enigma. At other times it is robed in bizarre apocalyptic garb. But always it is found in the embrace of the holy mystery that tells us:

"See, I am making all things new." (Rev 21:5)

"The first things have passed away"

As strange as the Book of Revelation might seem to many today, it sketches the contours of the ultimate goal of all creation and the threshold through which each individual must pass in

---

[4] See Duncan Reid, "Setting aside the Ladder to Heaven: Revelation 21:1–22:5 from the Perspective of the Earth," in *The Earth Bible*, vol. 1, *Reading from the Perspective of Earth,* ed. Norman C. Habel (Sheffield, UK: Sheffield Academic Press, 2000), 232–45.

order to realize that goal. So often in human life a clear picture of a goal enables the one striving for it to endure hardship in order to achieve it. This is not the case with the goal sketched in Revelation, or in other New Testament books for that matter. Paul admits:

For now we see in a mirror, dimly. (1 Cor 13:12)

Though eschatological fulfillment is spoken of as a new age, it is not time bound. Nor are new heavens and new Earth spatially conditioned. It is because Earth and all the members of the community of Earth are bound to space and time that our ultimate fulfillment is spoken of in terms of space and time. Despite the limitations of the literary expression, Revelation assures us that our ultimate fulfillment in all of its radicalism transcends and transforms but does not disdain what is earthly.

The ecojustice principles that have been employed as interpretive lenses throughout this book were devised to consider Earth and the members of the community of Earth in what apocalyptic eschatology understands as this age, the age of space and time as we know it. However, apocalyptic eschatology is really concerned with the age to come, the experience of transformation, an experience the essence of which we cannot grasp. Still, there is one point of which we can be sure: the radical transformation promised as eschatological fulfillment is not antagonist toward Earth and its components. Rather, it is actually the force that brings Earth to that fulfillment. The cosmic upheavals, the plagues, and the destruction of life that compose the visions in Revelation may be considered by some as punishment for wickedness, but the New Testament writers see them as the birthpangs of the messianic age. Revelation assures us that nothing of Earth is lost. Rather, all is transformed. One might say that the ecojustice principles are no longer goals to be achieved. They have now been realized.

Perhaps a far better way of viewing this vision of eschatological fulfillment is through the thinking of the great Jesuit theologian and scientist Pierre Teilhard de Chardin.[5] Teilhard

---

[5] Pierre Teilhard de Chardin (1881–1955) was a Jesuit priest-theologian and a distinguished geologist-paleontologist. Silenced by the

argued that the universe is evolving, not static. He maintained that all of creation is moving toward a point of convergence that he called the Omega Point. Though this Omega Point is the final convergence of all, it is also somehow the motivating force that from the beginning has directed everything toward convergence. Though he arrived at his understanding of this Omega Point through science, he found in Paul's concept of the cosmic Christ a way of bringing his scientific insights into line with his religious belief. For Teilhard, Christ is the point of ultimate convergence, the Omega Point.

Teilhard's perspective certainly finds correspondence in the final vision found in Revelation. Although this biblical book does not address questions regarding the physical evolution of the universe, it does follow the elements of that universe as they endure the birthpangs through which they must move in order to be born into newness *(kainós)*. Revelation portrays the final step in the emerging of the universe. Teilhard had a passionate love for the universe. This love sprang from his deep respect for power and beauty that shine through every aspect of it, a power and beauty that he saw as merely a reflection of the Creator. Paul possessed this insight as well, as did the author of Revelation.

Finally, while most of the Bible's eschatological tradition consists of promise and expectation, it is in the final vision of the Book of Revelation that we behold the ultimate manifestation of how God so loved the *kósmos*.

Vatican for his radical thinking, his writing was finally published after his death.

Conclusion

This book is called an experiment in hermeneutics. It offers an alternative lens through which to read and interpret the biblical tradition. New insights gleaned from contemporary cosmological discoveries have called us to look anew at our biblical tradition, a tradition grounded in the cosmology of the Ancient Near Eastern world. Contemporary cosmological insights have challenged us to refashion our understanding of theology accordingly. This is a pressing issue because many previous readings of biblical passages have supported the exploitation of Earth. Many ecosensitive individuals even insist that the biblical tradition itself is responsible for the devastation of the natural world, and therefore it should be discarded. Others argue that the anti-Earth perspectives spring from Ancient Near Eastern cultural limitations or biases, while the fundamental religious message can be retrieved and rehabilitated. The present book has sought to discover whether or not such retrieval is possible.

Various biblical texts have been examined in order to see whether they are ecofriendly or anti-Earth. The texts were chosen, not because they conformed to any ecojustice principles, but because they contained themes that correspond to some of the theology in the major sections of the Bible. The primary lens through which these texts were read was drawn from six ecojustice principles. In some instances the acknowledged cultural limitations and biases could be set aside and a new reading of the text was possible. At other times troublesome concepts appear to be inherent in the religious understanding and not merely in cultural perspectives.

What has this experiment uncovered? First, even a cursory reading shows that the Bible is concerned with human striving for righteous living and human faithfulness in relationship with God. These are certainly anthropocentric aspirations and might

suggest that all important biblical matters center on human beings. However, a more careful reading lays bare a fundamental
theological perspective. It shows that God is the primary focus
of this human striving; God initiates the covenant relationships;
and God determines the character of human faithfulness. In
other words God is at the center of the biblical tradition, not
human beings.

As mentioned above, the themes treated here were chosen
because of their importance. Chapter 1 traced the wandering of
ancient Israel's ancestors as recorded in the Pentateuch. It showed
that the routes chosen by these ancestors was influenced by the
accessibility of water. The indispensability of this element of
Earth underscores two major ecojustice principles: an appreciation of its intrinsic value and the interconnectedness of all members of the community of Earth. Chapter 2 examined passages
from the Historical Books in which attention was paid to the
various ways land was perceived. Always considered a gift from
God, land was prized as an inheritance allotted to ancestors and
handed down within the kinship structure. Because it was really
God's land, Israel was not to presume autonomous proprietary
rights over it but was responsible for its care. Viewing land in this
way underscores the ecojustice principle of intrinsic value. Furthermore, the practice of land sabbath acknowledges the delicate
balance that sustains the members of the community of Earth.

The "land flowing with milk and honey" was also a temptation for Israel. Examples of this were treated in Chapter 3.
The greed and exploitation condemned by the prophet Amos
scorned the human dignity of the poor people who suffered
from such injustice. Their intrinsic value was disdained; their
interconnectedness with other members of the community of
Earth was disparaged; and interdependence within the human
community was disregarded. The prophet Hosea denounced the
people's attempt to master and manipulate forces within the dynamic cosmic design that are under the control of God and not
human genius. The Wisdom tradition, which was discussed in
Chapter 4, provides direction for successful human living. While
there is certainly an anthropocentric dimension in such an approach, this tradition shows that successful living is found only
in human compliance with the dynamic cosmic design. It insists

that, as important as human beings might be, they are only one component of the much broader community of life. Thus, the Wisdom tradition promotes the principles of interconnectedness, interdependence, and mutual custodianship.

Everything in the New Testament developed out of the conviction that Jesus is the fulfillment of Jewish religious expectation and that the meaning of the entire cosmos is found in him. Aspects of this conviction as found in the Gospels were examined in Chapter 5. This examination showed that the demythologizing of the Christmas star and the disturbances of Earth that are reported in accounts of the crucifixion need not challenge the religious meaning that undergirds such reports. Rather, it calls for a more contemporary way of expressing that message. Furthermore, questioning the historical verity of miracles invites us to appreciate how God works through the laws and forces of nature rather than outside them. What's more, the use of nature parables in teaching religious truth suggests an inherent correspondence between elements in the broader natural world and aspects of human life. Finally, various products of nature, such as bread, possess profound symbolic value because human survival is dependent on them. Ecojustice principles of intrinsic value, interconnectedness, interdependence, and mutual custodianship are all reflected in these readings.

Paul's theology, as seen in Chapter 6, stems from his unshakable belief in the power of Jesus's death and resurrection. According to him, it is this power that situates Christ as both the firstborn of all creation and its ultimate fulfillment. Paul was convinced that there is a dynamic cosmic design, and Christ is its blueprint. Such a cosmological perspective faithfully embraces all of the ecojustice principles that have directed the present book. Finally, Revelation, the subject of Chapter 7, describes the transition from this age to the age of ultimate fulfillment and the glories of the transformation that awaits all creation. The majestic scenario that it paints reflects all of the ecojustice principles presented here.

Lest we think that every aspect of the biblical tradition is Earth friendly, we must note certain negative findings. The most prominent of these is the characterization of the land as a possession seized from the Canaanites already living on it. This study has shown that all the ecojustice principles are violated in the stories that belong to this tradition. Furthermore, the characterization of a deity who would direct, even command, people to act in such a way is troublesome, to say the least. Despite efforts to rehabilitate this tradition, problems persist. Perhaps all we can do is to maintain that the tradition of land as possession is historically conditioned by the cultural practices and understandings of that time rather than revelatory for all times.

A second negative finding is seen in Revelation's depiction of natural disaster as the punishment sent by an avenging God. While a cursory reading might lead to this understanding, interpreting the passages within Revelation's focus of apocalyptic eschatological fulfillment will enable the reader to recognize these events and their related suffering as examples of the birthpangs of the messianic age. In this way what appears at first glance as an anti-Earth perspective can be interpreted as Earth moving through the painful process toward transformation.

And so this experiment in hermeneutics comes to a close. Passages have been examined; results have been evaluated. The venture appears to have merit. Other interpreters are invited to step in and carry on.

Further Reading

Achtemeier, Paul J. *Romans* in *Interpretation: A Bible Commentary for Teaching and Preaching*. Atlanta: John Knox Press, 1985.

Bauckham, Richard. *The Bible and Ecology: Rediscovering the Community of Creation*. Waco, TX: Baylor University Press, 2010.

Brown, Raymond E., SS. *The Birth of the Messiah*, The Anchor Bible Reference Library. New York: Doubleday, 1992.

Coloe, Mary L., ed. *Creation Is Groaning: Biblical and Theological Perspectives*. Collegeville, MN: Liturgical Press, 2013.

Edwards, Denis. "Exploring How God Acts." In *God, Grace, and Creation*, College Theology Society Annual Volume, no. 55, ed. Philip J. Rossi. Maryknoll, NY: Orbis Books, 2010.

Fretheim, Terence E. *Creation Untamed: The Bible, God, and Natural Disasters*. Grand Rapids, MI: Baker Academic, 2010.

Habel, Norman C. *An Inconvenient Text*. Adelaide, AUC: ATF Press, 2009.

Habel, Norman C., ed. *Reading from the Perspective of Earth*. Vol. 1 in *The Earth Bible*. Cleveland, OH: The Pilgrim Press, 2000.

———. *The Earth Story in the Psalms and the Prophets*. Vol. 4 in *The Earth Bible*. Cleveland, OH: The Pilgrim Press, 2000.

Habel, Norman C., and Vicky Balabanski, eds. *The Earth Story in the New Testament*. Vol. 5 in *The Earth Bible*. Cleveland, OH: The Pilgrim Press, 2000.

Habel, Norman C., and Peter Trudinger, eds. *Exploring Ecological Hermeneutics*. Atlanta: Society of Biblical Literature, 2008.

Habel, Norman C., and Shirley Wurst, eds. *The Earth Bible in Genesis*. Vol. 2 in *The Earth Bible*. Cleveland, OH: The Pilgrim Press, 2000.

————. *The Earth Story in Wisdom Traditions*. Vol. 3 in *The Earth Bible*. Cleveland, OH: The Pilgrim Press, 2001.

Harrington, Wilfrid J., OP. *Revelation* in *Sacra Pagina*, no 16. Collegeville, MN: Liturgical Press, 1993.

Horrell, David G. *Bible and the Environment: Towards a Critical Ecological Biblical Theology*. London, UK: Equinox, 2010.

King, Philip J., and Lawrence E. Stager. *Life in Biblical Israel*. Louisville, KY: Westminster John Knox, 2001.

Leopold, Aldo. *A Sand County Almanac: And Sketches Here and There*. New York: Oxford University Press, 1949.

Lovelock, James. *Gaia: A New Look at Life on Earth*. 3rd ed. New York: Oxford University Press, 2000.

Lowery, Richard H. *Sabbath and Jubilee*. St. Louis, MO: Chalice Press, 2000.

Macky, Peter W. *The Centrality of Metaphors to Biblical Thought: A Method for Interpreting the Bible*. Lewiston, NY: The Edward Mellen Press, 1990.

Margulis, Lynn. *Symbiotic Planet: A New Look at Evolution*. New York: Basic Books, 1998.

White, Lynn. "The Religious Roots of Our Ecological Crisis." *Science* 155 (1967): 1203–7.

Index